TRUMP

CHOSEN ONE

Art of Leadership, Influence, and Empowerment

Durollari

Published and Copyright @ 2019 by Durollari
ISBN: 9781702250634
Imprint: Independently published

I dedicated this book to my grandmother Demire, my mother Nedime, along with my father Dr. Guri, and my lovely eternal princess Dbborra.

Table of Content

REMARKS OF PRESIDENT DONALD J. TRUMP – AS PREPARED FOR DELIVERY

INAUGURAL ADDRESS

FRIDAY, JANUARY 20, 2017

WASHINGTON, D.C.

As Prepared for Delivery

Chief Justice Roberts, President Carter, President Clinton, President Bush, President Obama, fellow Americans, and people of the world: thank We, the citizens of America, are now joined in a great national effort to rebuild our country and to restore its promise for all of our people. Together, we will determine the course of America and the world for years to come. We will face challenges. We will confront hardships. But we will get the job done.

Every four years, we gather on these steps to carry out the orderly and peaceful transfer of power, and we are grateful to President Obama and First Lady Michelle Obama for their gracious aid throughout this transition. They have been magnificent.

Today's ceremony, however, has very special meaning. Because today we are not merely transferring power from one Administration to another, or from one party to another – but we are transferring power from Washington, D.C. and giving it back to you., the American People.

For too long, a small group in our nation's Capital has reaped the rewards of government while the people have borne the cost. Washington flourished – but the people did not share in its wealth. Politicians prospered – but the jobs left, and the factories closed.

The establishment protected itself, but not the citizens of our country. Their victories have not been victories; their triumphs have not been triumphs; and while they celebrated in our nation's Capital, there was little to celebrate for struggling families across our land.

That all changes – starting right here, and right now, because this moment is your moment: it belongs to you.

It belongs to everyone gathered here today and everyone watching across America. This is your day. This is your celebration. And this, the United States of America, is your country. What truly matters is not which party controls our government, but whether our government is controlled by the people.

January 20th, 2017 will be remembered as the day the people became the rulers of this nation again. The forgotten men and women of our country will be forgotten no longer. Everyone is listening to you. Now you came by the tens of millions to become part of a historic movement the likes of which the world has never seen before. At the center of this movement is a crucial conviction: that a nation exists to serve its citizens.

Americans want great institutions for their people, safe neighborhoods for their families, and good jobs for themselves. These are the just and reasonable demands of a righteous public. But for too many of our citizens, a different reality exists: Mothers and people trapped in poverty in our inner cities; rusted-out factories scattered like tombstones across the landscape of our nation; an system, flush with cash, but which leaves our .ng and beautiful people deprived of knowledge; and the crime and gangs and drugs that have stolen too many lives and robbed our country of so much unrealized potential.

This American carnage stops right here and stops right now. We are one nation – and their pain is our pain. Their dreams are our dreams; and their success will be our success. We share one heart, one home, and one glorious destiny.

The oath of office I take today is an oath of allegiance to all Americans. For many decades, we've enriched foreign industry at the expense of American industry; Subsidized the armies of other countries while allowing for the very sad depletion of our military; We've defended other nation's borders while refusing to defend our own; And spent trillions of dollars overseas while America's infrastructure has fallen into disrepair and decay.

We've made other countries rich while the wealth, strength, and confidence of our country has disappeared over the horizon. One by one, the factories shuttered and left our shores, with not even a thought about the millions upon millions of American workers left behind. The wealth of our middle class has been ripped from their homes and then redistributed across the entire world. But that is the past. And now we are looking only to the future.

We assembled here today are issuing a new decree to be heard in every city, in every foreign capital, and in every hall of power. From this day forward, a new vision will govern our land. From this moment on, it's going to be America First. Every decision on trade, on taxes, on immigration, on foreign affairs, will be made to benefit American workers and American families.

We must protect our borders from the ravages of other countries making our products, stealing our companies, and destroying our jobs. Protection will lead to great prosperity and strength. I will fight for you. with every breath in my body – and I will never, ever let you down.

America will start winning again, winning like never before. We will bring back our jobs. We will bring back our borders. We will bring back our wealth. And we will bring back our dreams. We will build new roads, and highways, and bridges, and airports, and tunnels, and railways all across our wonderful nation.

We will get our people off of welfare and back to work – rebuilding our country with American hands and American labor. We will follow two simple rules: Buy American and Hire American. We will seek friendship and goodwill with the nations of the world – but we do so with the understanding that it is the right of all nations to put their own interests first.

We do not seek to impose our way of life on anyone, but rather to let it shine as an example for everyone to follow. We will reinforce old alliances and form new ones – and unite the civilized world against Radical Islamic Terrorism, which we will eradicate completely from the face of the Earth. At the bedrock of our politics will be a total allegiance to the United States of America, and through our loyalty to our country, we will rediscover our loyalty to each other. When you. open your heart to patriotism, there is no room for prejudice.

The scriptures tell us, "how good and pleasant it is when God's people live together in unity." We must speak our minds openly, debate our disagreements honestly, but always pursue solidarity. When America is united, America is totally unstoppable. There should be no fear – we are protected, and we will always be protected. We will be protected by the great men and women of our military and law enforcement and, most importantly, we are protected by God.

Finally, we must think big and dream even bigger. In America, we understand that a nation is only living as long as it is striving. We will no longer accept politicians who are all talk and no action – constantly complaining but never doing anything about it. The time for empty talk is over. Now arrives the hour of action. Do not let anyone tell you. it cannot be done. No challenge can match the heart and fight and spirit of America.

We will not fail. Our country will thrive and prosper again. We stand at the birth of a new millennium, ready to unlock the mysteries of space, to free the Earth from the miseries of disease, and to harness the energies, industries, and technologies of tomorrow. A new national pride will stir our souls, lift our sights, and heal our divisions.

It is time to remember that old wisdom our soldiers will never forget: that whether we are black or brown or white, we all bleed the same red blood of patriots, we all enjoy the same glorious freedoms, and we all salute the same great American Flag.

And whether a child is born in the urban sprawl of Detroit or the windswept plains of Nebraska, they look up at the same night sky, they fill their heart with the same dreams, and they are infused with the breath of life by the same almighty Creator. So, to all Americans, in every city near and far, small and large, from mountain to mountain, and from ocean to ocean, hear these words:

You. will never be ignored again. your, voice, your hopes, and your dreams, will define our American destiny. And your courage and goodness and love will forever guide us along the way. Together, We Will Make America Strong Again. We Will Make America Wealthy Again. We Will Make America Proud Again. We Will Make America Safe Again. And, Yes, Together, We Will Make America Great Again. Thank you., God Bless you., And God Bless America.

Notes:

Political and Social Relevance of the Scriptures

"Trump Chosen One" is a further examination into the relevance of biblical ideology and intervention into the fabric of American politics and society and the impact of a globalist ideology and master plan towards world dominance in all aspects of humanity to include, social, political, religious and suppression of free speech and expression.

The focus of the CHOSEN ONE is to discover how to implement ancient biblical philosophy into today's new contemporary thinking and ideology of faith as they relate to political and business leaders around the world.

Introducing biblical debate in professional settings has the potential to provide for the intelligent analysis of the scriptures while offering an interdisciplinary dialogue between biblical scholars, philosophers, and scientific experts, and political leaders.

Human civilization has reached a global crisis with machines replacing the human workforce, automating goods and services surpassing human work capability thousand-fold. Technology is responsible for the production of an abundance never witnessed before in human history, resulting in a shift employment opportunity across the global market. The displacement of all the employment trends has been indirectly responsible for the current uprisings in the Middle East, with the never-ending wars causing standards of living inequality and rampant poverty and overall poor conditions created by the globalist, warmongering agenda and local, corrupt regional governments.

In order to address the global inequalities, biblical principles with integrity, moral, and just ideology can fill the void by offering a contemporary approach in using the scriptures as an emerging discipline of public theology and relevance in addressing today's global crisis. This global crisis calls for political leaders to take the lead to integrate biblical theology into many aspects of governance and society. For example, in today's American political scene, we are witnessing the perversion of language and a corrupt and unjust justice system of politics of the political structure, the use of lies deceit and corrupt investigations based on false testimony and deceit.

The Russian meddling and Ukraine investigation into President Trump and his associates is a tactical operation coordinated between multiple government intelligence agencies, global corporations, politicians, and many media outlets designed to undo the 2016 elections and unseat President Trump from office. These treasonous acts by unelected officials and corrupt media further reinforce the existence of a shadow government consisting of career employees and their associates, highlighting a dual justice system for the general public and another for the social and political elite. This dual justice system is very apparent, as highlighted with the takedown of Trump associate, with FBI raids reserved for high profile criminals and drug lords, the takedown included ground, areal, and tactical sea invasion of the arrest of Roger Stone and others.

We are living in an upside-down world of a twisted reality that is full of lies and deceit painstakingly characterized as a runaway world manipulated by a shadow network of a globalist secret society. The world today does not reflect humanity's vision of how the world should be, rather than being more under the peoples' influence and control, it is being run by a power-hungry political class, in collusion with governmental agencies, banking systems, and global corporate giants.

Political leaders along with advances in technological advances and scientific breakthroughs were supposed to have a predictable and positive influence in our lives; instead, it has produced an opposite effect of a conglomerate network of data collection and privacy infringements that are controlling humanities daily activities that are directly influencing a future of unpredictability and an out of control and a runaway ruling class. Continuous wars and destruction in today's world are the cause of the collapse of many countries and nations, with millions of lost lives with a path of destruction and a downward spiral of human sacrifice and significant catastrophic events looming at a moment's notice.

The last century has served humanity well with improvements across the board in many sectors, to include space exploration, medicine, and technological advances. Additionally, human equality and standards of living have dramatically improved with advances in the energy sector. The political arena continues to struggle and advance in a more rational civil manner, with a continuous discourse and ideology between the Democratic and Republican parties.

The ideological differences between both parties, along with the visionary roadmap towards the future are on opposite spectrums, with no compromise in sight. A scorched earth strategy by the social far-left movement relies on the Stalinist approach towards political dominance, as recent attacks and false accusations and testimony against the Trump administration with a constant barrage of offensive posture and threats of impeachment with no legal justification or real evidence of wrongdoing. Stalin once said, "show me the man, and then I will show. The crime," this communist approach is currently being used by the Democratic party of the United States of America to frame President Trump, working and colluding with intelligence moles planted in the White House and other government agencies.

First, there was a Russian collusion delusion, and now it is the Ukrainian dirt and collection of information on political opponents' nonsense, secret closed-door investigations conducted in highly secure governmental facilities with no opportunities or scrutiny for oversight. Now, the question remains for the American public, will people sit back and allow the destruction of governmental institutions with ideologically bankrupt and legally corrupt leftist politician class continue their vicious cycle bent on the destruction of not only the Presidency but also the will of the American public. While the President is under one phony investigation after another by the leftist of the democratic party members along with their coconspirators the fake news media attacks, unelected government employees, and mentally ill politicians and social elites, they are not only attacking the President, but they are also attacking the American people.

A Renaissance and awakening of the America human spirit to the truth must happen in order to maintain our leadership role in the world. Citizens of the world look at America as a beacon of freedom and equality and an example of a structured and working democracy with a

Constitution grounded in the faith and belief of a spiritual God and not the earthly kings or queens having dominion over the earth and its people.

With the recent announcement by President Trump, withdrawing forces from the Middle East was immediately scrutinized and objected by prominent leaders of both Democratic and Republican parties and political pundits. The opposition towards the never-ending wars demonstrates the political prostitution of many political leaders working on behalf of the military-industrial complex.

Politicians are not working on behalf of their constituents or in the interest of the people and are more interested in their agendas and financial benefit using political kickback schemes and phony charity organizations or using family members as props for payoffs for favors, political and business access.

The impact of the current political terrain and global transformation in technology for the last century further reinforces the need for the renaissance and rebirth along with the popularity and practices of biblical principles back into the mainstream of society. It is necessary to focus on the discipline of biblical studies for cultivating present and future intellectuals to intervene in political discourse while advocating the scriptures as a source for decisions concerning local and global issues.

Human civilization has reached a breaking point, with ineffective strategies used by highly regarded political leaders attempting to manage the world's conflicts and resources. Nations are in a constant stance of war with recent uprisings in the Middle East and other regions of the world, fighting for power and perceived shortages of resources. The current crises in the Middle East in effect are due to the inequality in standards of living with rampant poverty and overall poor conditions created by their corrupt governments.

Most people are a product of their environment, and if people are around corrupt and sick societies, they can, in turn, become a reflection of that society. On the opposite, if people lived in a wholesome environment based on the teachings of the scriptures, they would likely be peaceful and more productive global citizens.

In President Lincoln's second inaugural address he gives praise to The Lord, "We have been the recipients of the choicest bounties of Heaven; we have been preserved these many years in peace and prosperity; we have grown in numbers, wealth and power as no other nation has ever grown, we have forgotten God. We have forgotten the gracious hand which has preserved us in peace and multiplied and enriched and strengthened us, and we have vainly imagined, in the deceitfulness of our hearts, that all these blessings are of superior wisdom and virtue of our own. Intoxicated with unbroken success, we have become too self-sufficient to feel the necessity of redeeming and preserving grace, too proud to pray to the God that made us. It behooves us, then, to humble ourselves before the offended Power, to confess our national sins and to pray for clemency and forgiveness."

World leaders have an enormous responsibility on their shoulders; first, they must learn how to place their pride, and individual interest is aside, while at the same time coming to grips with the reality of their inability to control world events. Leaders have only to investigate the scriptures for answers; all they must do is rely on their faith and turn towards the scriptures for wisdom and the truth. The scriptures provide human civilization with a historical legacy, not only of past events but as an actual living source that can be used today and well into the future.

Religious inspiration can serve world leaders well in creating policies and laws based on the words of God, and not some false ideological manifestation created by an evil man, for starters world leaders continue to resist solving the current multifaceted global crisis while proposing alternative solutions that directly are not working and only benefit a few corporate leaders in their quest of monopolizing the world's natural resources. God has created our earthly domain in such a way that man will never be able to master his history unless man submits to Him fully and lives in harmony with nature and his surroundings. World leaders must attempt to identify the root causes that have created this critical situation of rampant ecological and human destruction with no end in sight. Humanity continues the path of self-destruction; drastic changes need to happen now in order to divert a global catastrophe.

The exponential growth in technological advances and knowledge has shifted the power base to a few developed nations. Modern society continues to struggle with political unrest, and ecological destruction while maintaining control over the world continues to be elusive for the world's leaders. The better world promised by advances in technology and science has not arrived, rather uncertainty and inequality are in present danger threatening humanity every day. Human ignorance has made the destruction of every living thing to disappear in a flash. Moreover, knowledge has opened the way towards a more patient population, with diversity in cultural and religious beliefs and rapid spreading of democracy. The world is going through a transformation affecting every part of our lives and is leaning towards establishing one global order.

The new world order consists of most of the world's influential individuals, along with their political control in many continents. The new world order orchestrated by the world's superpowers aims at uniting nations to secure global peace and security for everyone. The new world order agenda seems to provide several influential individuals or groups with control over many countries' resources and political leaders. President Lincoln warns leaders not to think of themselves as godly because of their status, "It is the duty of nations as well as of men to own their dependence upon the overruling power of God, and to confess their sins and transgressions in humble sorrow, yet with assured hope that genuine repentance will lead to mercy and pardon, and to recognize the sublime truth, announced in Holy Scripture, and proven by all history, that those nations only are blessed whose God is the Lord." The biblical scriptures continue to warn leaders of establishing total domination and control of the world with a new world order, thus replacing God with false demigods as described in Revelations.

Religious circles have always advocated the integration of the scriptures in all aspects of society to include studies influencing social behaviour and global strategy. Theological/religious debate requires official forums in government and professional al settings. These forums will make it possible for civil debate, while further sparking critical thinking and decision-making processes. Religious debate is a form of an intellectual model for leaders to emulate and make part of their daily work environment. Leaders must remember that their decisions affect present and future generations and are part of the reality of a global risk society.

For this reason, religious leaders must adequately present their case of interpreting the ancient text of the scriptures and make it relevant to the needs of the global risk society today. Integrating the scriptures in the social fabric of a global society can immensely contribute to the peaceful advancement of human civilization. In Deuteronomy 16:1 -25:19 Moses provides a future direction, by furnishing clear guidelines for his nation's future. Considering the historical struggle between the Protestant Reformation and the Catholic Church clear guidelines and vision for religious followers continues to be intertwined in a web of deceit and confusion.

A major stumbling block for advancing religiosity into the mainstream of society has been the lack of initiatives to incorporate any relevance to public life and the present business market. Religious leaders must always look for opportunities to educate the public in a way that any individual can realize the fullest potential of the scriptures in improving their quality of personal life and work environment. The integration of the scriptures into mainstream society would require a paradigm shift in attitude and behavioral change to accept the ways of the Lord into their hearts and souls. With the newfound wisdom and knowledge learned from the scriptures, humanity would be better prepared to deal with the ecological and human crisis in a more ethical way following the scriptures.

In a tale of two cities, Charles Dickens wrote, "It was the best of times; it was the worst of times." We live in exciting times, with discoveries almost daily and improvements to our living standards never imagined before. Nevertheless, something continues to be out of place and not seem right; this may be due to humankind distancing himself from his Creator, The Lord.

Religious leaders can no longer remain within their comfort zones of their parish, while only surrounding themselves with like-minded people. Introducing biblical studies to the political arenas and especially university settings is a natural progression towards social and nation-building. Biblical studies, as of recent, have gained some interest by people and intellectuals and particularly non-faith-based individuals and groups throughout many parts of the globe. The scriptures serve as a great resource of wisdom and knowledge that can only benefit the individual and governments in developing health policies and addressing social issues while attempting to establish some normalcy. The scriptures provide a significant amount of information devoted to the approaches of teaching and apprentices that Jesus used to instruct his followers. Scholars continue to investigate the methods of teaching Jesus used, with the use of parables, allegory, rhetoric, prophecy, and numerous other teaching methods.

Religiosity involves faithful and more intuit understanding of natural surroundings, which is experienced and developed with dedicated devotion to the faith. The integration of the scriptures into the political decision-making process has been challenging to achieve for the last few centuries, especially with a negative cloud surrounding the dark history of the middle ages in Europe and the ecclesiastical inquisitions murdering thousands for heresy.

Many countries have adopted separation of the church and state policies in order not to repeat the mistakes of the past. Placing complete control of the scriptures under the rule of a few select leaders or dictators leaves the potential for corruption and manipulation, while individuals lose the direct relationship with God. The First Amendment to the Constitution states that "Congress shall make no law respecting an establishment of religion or prohibiting the free exercise thereof." The ideal is for everyone to study and debate the scriptures on their own accord and not rely upon others to dictate the Word of God. The question remains, how should biblical studies be approached and be made relevant in politics and everyday life?

Scriptures study an intelligent and caring approach in being introduced to mainstream society, political arenas, and al settings. Religious groups or individuals of faith need not be overbearing in their approach but must take a balanced approach in allowing for intelligent debate and conversation. It is human nature to resist when faced with unfamiliar concepts and ideas, especially when it comes to an understanding of the scriptures considering the problematic situation posed by different interpretations and sources. The scriptures do provide much room for debate, while intelligent debate can be a vehicle for understanding and allowing the truth to surface. The political powers of the world cannot ignore the issue of concurrent use of the biblical as an emerging discipline of public theology and relevance in addressing global inequalities and conflicts. The need to design biblical theology relevance to local and global institutions is imminent. The task calls for the integration of biblical theology into many spears of society with interdisciplinary crossover into many different studies. The next logical step to consider would be the relationship between God and leaders, political officials, and religious leaders. The most critical ingredient for the success of biblical lessons crossing over between the groups is flexibility in learning and sharing of experience and knowledge. It is learning decisions with the central theme as God being part of the relationship that exists in reaching the ultimate goals of the parties involved.

In the last few decades, there has been an increased concern for the establishment of a more sustained interdisciplinary dialogue between biblical scholars and philosophers of many disciplines. In this research article, aimed at leaders in a global sense and public masses, offering a descriptive and historical overview of biblical study can cross over and establish a presence in the decision-making process concerning local and global issues.

The aim of the integration of scriptures is finding ways of bridging the gap between relevant religious philosophy and contemporary thinking and methodology in addressing the crisis in today's global society. As with any movement, and especially establishing a biblical presence in society, will be met with resistance from philosophers, scholars, and political figures to maintain the stronghold of separation between church and state. Whatever the mixed, Religious leaders must stay on course in spreading the gospels while demonstrating an appreciation for the fundamental Religious doctrine and philosophy. It is apparent that world leaders are not capable of finding lasting solutions to the global crisis facing human civilization, and the right solutions seem to point towards the Words of God. Will man be capable of diverting the epic biblical catastrophe or continuing the path of a godless world and self-destruction?

Notes:

Leadership Character Analysis

Trump the Chosen One teaches leaders should have high moral, ethical standards of character and principles; they must have a high moral character with a vision towards the future. Leaders affect the lives of many people, and they must be big-picture thinkers while leading with a worldly view. They must continually seek the truth and knowledge in order to create an environment of a spiritual and rewarding experience for the people they lead. The role of al leaders plays in character building, not only for themselves but also for the people under their influence. It is apparent that many questions the integrity and moral charter of many of today's leaders, not only in but all spectrums of society. Leaders are challenged to be positive role models while demonstrating strong character with high morals and integrity in everything they do.

Building al Leaders of Tomorrow

The hierarchical structure and politics have created rigid empires that are inflexible in implementing changes to meet the current demands of their people and society's needs. Governmental powers are mainly concerned with their scope of interest, while many questions the ethical practices of these institutions and the character of the leaders. While many leaders are heartfelt and want to provide the people with the best possible, there are exceptions, and many are more concerned with their interests. The problem may lay not in the efforts of the leaders, but on the system as a whole and the ethical stance of these institutions to include the character and authority of their leaders. For example, concerning a leader's authority, King Solomon issues a warning, "when leaders try to exercise authority without a servant's heart, they eventually hurt themselves. Leaders add value by serving others" Ecclesiastes 8:1-9., Leaders must be individuals of vision and faith while putting people first above their ambitions and interests. Trump is demonstrating, every day, by his actions in love of country, duty, and placing the needs of the people above all else.

Leaders such as Trump create a positive environment for their people while implementing changes that are sound with proven theory and experimentation, with priority on continuous improvement initiatives, such as President regulations reduction initiatives and much more sound governmental process improvement across many sectors and programs.

Solomon once said, 'we do not control the timing of most events; the best we can do is to recognize the timing" Ecclesiastes 3:1-8.,

Trump has turned the established order upside down, with initiatives aimed at improving the lives of the people. Trump knows the world is continuously moving and changing at a rapid pace; he is taking bold initiatives needed in order to face the challenges of today and the future. Integrating sound and just decision making is creating a winning environment throughout many industrial and social sectors. Using scientific data and logical and sound decision making is producing exceptional results in the economy and other sectors of government and society.

Our conscience and our central neural system plugged into the artificial intelligence may someday provide us with better ideas in order to maximize our creativity and individuality. The system should stress the importance of science, coupled with the role and balance of faith. We all are born with unlimited potential from the first day of birth; the challenge is to break down barriers and limitations we artificially place. God has given us an incredible machine, our conscience that can take us anywhere our imagination would go.

Many institutions are more of a reflection of an authoritarian system with dictatorship acts rewarded while creativity and high moral character are set asides. The system rewards most obedient individuals that go along with the flow and do not rock the boat, completely ignoring the essential traits of character and integrity. Individuals that do not adopt or follow the rules are either fired or given fewer responsibilities.

Many questions continue, for example, are the institutions' system concerned about the individual or the interest of its existence and their bottom line. According to Proverbs on ants and leadership, "Ants do not need a commander to tell them to get started. Ants work faithfully and need no outside accountability to keep them doing the right. Ants work hard and will replace their anthill when it gets ruined" Proverbs 6:6-8., Leaders need to allow people to be able to use their creativity and freedom of expression for them to grow spiritually and professionally.

Freedom, our God-given right must be protected at all costs at the same time limiting the power of governments, balanced between total authoritarian and anarchy.

Motivational Leadership

Each person has a different personality style with varied learning and development abilities. These individual differences come in the form of intelligence and creativity; each one of us has a different capacity to process information and how we relate to one another. Motivation and attitude determine success; it is an internal state of mind that guides us towards higher achievement and goals. Solomon says, "he observes a person in a variety of contexts, and nothing seems to satisfy them" Ecclesiastes 4:1-8. Successful leaders find ways to motivate people by capturing their level of interest and by building their confidence along with allowing then the freedom to express themselves.

Intrinsic motivation comes from internal factors that are within and can be controlled by the effort and devotion to the goal or task placed by the individual. On the other hand, extrinsic motivations are external factors that come in the form of reward and punishment that are outside the individual control. These motivation techniques are just part of the tools required for effective leadership and management of any situation or position of command. Individuals in a position of authority need to have a breadth of experience in many areas of leadership principles, management, and psychology and especially personality typing training. We all have different personalities, and the most effective leaders realize this and change their style of leading to fit the situation. For example, when new trainees with a little experience, the more direct approach, while highly trained professions require a participated approach and style that would be a better fit.

According to King Solomon, while observing people, he noticed the following concerning what motivates them, "They need comfort and fulfilment, completion and triumph, and consumption and greed" Ecclesiastes 4:1-8. There is a lot more to leadership than meets the eye, it takes many years' experience and training in leadership and developing the whole person concept to be practical and understanding people and what makes them tick.

It was fortunate to have had many different leadership positions in the military to hone technical and management and leadership skills and continuously retool approach to dealing with people of different cultures and backgrounds. Sure, it has made the share of mistakes along the way and realized and what has helped the training coupled with theories I learned throughout the years. To be able to try out many theories and to find out what worked – one of the most effective management tools a leader can use is personality typing, not only makes understand people around better, but it also makes one learn about oneself, and that is the key towards a more successful leader.

Conclusion

Successful leaders, such as Trump, realize it is tough to control or change people around them, especially with all the leaks. Sure, leaders can use their power and authority over them, but this is not real leadership. Leadership is when one turns on back, and people will do the right thing because they want to not because they must. The most important thing to realize as a leader is to adjust personality to fit the situation and the individual. Leaders need to be highly ethical individuals with higher standards of integrity and moral values. They in a position of authority that has lasting effects for the people they lead. It is essential for leaders to look at positive examples and not to abuse their authority and always stay humble to their approach when dealing with the people under them.

Teach character? Good leaders demonstrate it by leading by example. Successful leaders lead by example, and for example, General Patton once said, "One is on parade every day" the people under command will observe every move and action taken; therefore, it is essential to be the best example can be. Character is something that is gained from an early age and influenced by family, friends, society, and personality. Most of us are born with a sound mind, and we intrinsically know from right and wrong, look at it comes down to making a choice. Character comes to play, especially when faced with making hard decisions. Will choose the route of least resistance or will make the right decision based on a strong character based on leadership traits of high integrity, honesty, and courage.

Notes:

God's Plan for Leadership:

A Communication Perspective, and Leadership Challenge.

Leaders should strive towards more significant personal and

professional standards with the highest ethical and moral characteristics possible. Leaders touch the lives of many, and for this, they must be wise thinkers with a vision towards the future, leading with a worldly view. Leaders must create a spiritual and rewarding environment for their people. This research paper investigates the characteristics and traits of being a successful leader. Successful leaders demonstrate a high level of integrity, loyalty, selflessness, and decisiveness.

Additionally, great leaders have a God-given ability to influence, motivate, and educate their followers. Leaders must challenge themselves in being the best leaders they can be, demonstrating leadership in action based on faith, integrity, and the moral obligation for the betterment of the people under their command. It is reasonable to assume that character and personality traits are associated with leadership, while others are not. Society places heavy emphasis on character and leadership qualities and then associates them with success, but it is interesting to understand the failures of leadership as well. Some leaders forget about the goal and concentrate on themselves instead of the whole. Good leaders understand the importance of good communications; followers need to know the plan, and they need to know.

God's plan provides leaders with a road map that includes people with a biblical worldview on how to train and educate their people following scriptures principles. Gods plan is defined as, "The life-long, scriptures-based, centered process of leading a people into a new identity with developing in according to his/her specific abilities given to him by higher power, so that a people would be empowered to live a life characterized by love, trust, and obedience to God." A kingdom not only reaffirms biblical teachings is also a philosophy on how religious should conduct their lives and train up based on God's kingdom.

God's kingdom as "His reign as King of Kings in a person's daily life," reaffirming that God is the rule maker and religious are the implementers.

Kingdom is Religious centered with God as the ultimate authority concerning all aspects of teaching and educating people with a biblical world view. Religious have the responsibility to adequately prepare, teach, and direct their people towards serving the Lord. Kingdom revolves around constantly reinforcing and building Religious values on people today and future generations while staying centered on God and the ultimate truth.

Kingdom can only survive and flourish if the Religious values and principles are taught continuously and reinforced to people at school, home, and church. A world view is at the core of the teaching profession; for example, in a communist society, the leader was required to pass on atheist and Darwinist theories to their people. The Religious world view encompasses a set of values based on an infinite God and stresses high standards of moral character. Leaders are entrusted with teaching and influencing people, and this why they must have a religious world view. Responsibility can not only fall on leaders, but it is also even more critical that parents be active partners in educating and being positive role models by demonstrating firm Religious values in order to help their people establish a strong character base. The Roman Empire fell because morality in the family decayed to the point of collapse under the rule of a humanistic dictatorship. Religious philosophy on the other hand of is primarily concerned about God's law and to ensure Biblical values are passed on to their people.

God's Word into practice. Leaders strongly stress that for the kingdom to have a chance in religious families, the scriptures must be studied and put into practice throughout their people's lives. Parents must keep in mind that it is easiest to teach people religious values during their early years and continue reinforcing them until maturity. As people learn the scriptures, it is essential for them not to memorize but to learn and apply the principles in daily life. Educating people should fall primarily on parents; they must uphold their responsibilities to teach and pass on knowledge requiring a fully dedicated Religious commitment. The primary goal of teaching the scriptures to people is to install a religious world view and a channel for spreading God's truth. With today's busy lifestyle and financial stresses on the family, both parents are required to work in most instances. Because of this many parents find it is easy to delegate the responsibility of raising and educating people to others. In Deuteronomy 6:7, it states, "And thou shalt teach them diligently unto thy people, and shalt talk of them when thou sittest in thine house, and when thou walkest by the way, and when thou liest down, and when thou risest up." religious must be attentive to delegating their responsibilities of bringing up their people to others, and they must do their part by watching and teaching their people 24/7.

Kingdom supports initiatives that require a teamwork approach that includes leaders, parents, church, and the community working together in spreading the Religious philosophy and world view to their people. The Religious community, overall, should ensure people continue and pass on God's truth to current and future generations. With the decline of Western society, the church and parents alike are incredibly concerned about the decline of religious values not only in society but also in the religious community. Religious leaders must have a big-picture view of world affairs, politics, and their surroundings in order to stay on the course of God's master plan. The last century has demonstrated the decline of the religious foothold on society, transitioning from a Religious/Scientific value perspective to a New Age attitude.

In the last century, they have brought about technological improvements across the board in many sectors to include space travel, medicine, and others to include religious philosophy. As technological improvements daily, religious beliefs have also evolved from a religious base to a New Age attitude consisting of a business-like model and attitude that requires constant evolution and change to fit the situation or needs of the times. With all the advances in technology, the evolution of politics, one would wonder that society would be further ahead at curbing violence and wars throughout the world. It is the incomprehensive view that political and the churches inactivity have not done much in stopping or curbing society's issues, and the only salvation may be a collective return to the scriptures for answers. Our current political and monetary systems are splitting at the seams and with rampant war and turmoil throughout most regions of the world. Nations are in a constant stance of war, fighting for resources to benefit a select a few; meanwhile, the world leaders and the church stand by, watching silently as the world turns even more violent with catastrophes looming at a moment's notice. A large portion is still living in a world of poverty while at the same time being enslaved by their corrupt governments and corporations. Humankind must return to the scriptures for answers, and the only saving grace is the truth based on the infinite God.

The western-style of leadership has proved challenging to implement into mainstream society in Europe and the Americas, as witnessed by today's and attitude of people towards religion. Many people today feel that religion should be an individual choice and not something that society should embrace. The Western attitude towards religion may stem from the teachings of ancient Greece and Roman philosophy, stressing more of the humanistic ideals. Even today, many parts of the people living in Europe and America enjoy excellent food, drink, and pleasure take priority over spiritual warship and the strict obedience required by the scriptures. The lack of religious connection may stem from the importation of the Hebrew scriptures into Western civilization. From an early age, Hebrew people learn about their faith and how to live and make the scriptures part of their culture that identifies them as the global Jewish community. Western civilization, on the other hand, adopted the Hebrew scriptures but continues to struggle with fully integrating them into their culture. Today, have no idea if someone is a true believer in God or a false prophet that is more concerned about becoming rich by using religion in order to satisfy his or her ego and surround themselves with more materialistic pleasures?

As a leader, it is essential to be aware of the political and religious struggles facing society today. The pillars and fabric of society, and the decisions concerning what and how people taught are not determined by parents but by political forces controlling the system and laws. In most instances, political leaders do not act on what is in favour of the people or parents but by what they and their constituents feel is right. People should have more of a say-so into the decision-making process concerning their social, legal, educational and many other issues to include what younger generations educated and what they learn and how they learn. The problem is that church leaders have not been an active partner in organizing more initiatives to bring God back into the classroom. It is also the parent's responsibility to elect leaders that they feel would support them and carry out their wishes. Public school leaders are placed in a challenging position and must obey the rules and regulations placed on them by Federal and state agencies.

Kouzes and Posner, in their book The Leadership Challenge, ask a question if leadership principles learned? An individual's personality developed approximately the age of seven, and each person has a different personality profile with varied learning and development abilities. These individual differences come in the form of intelligence and creativity; everyone has a different capacity to process information and how he/she relates to the environment and others. Do the old-age questions remain if leaders are born or made?

Individuals in any position of authority need to have a breadth of and experience in the areas of leadership and management coupled with the ability to use various psychological profiling techniques in order to be the best leaders they can be. Successful leaders have demonstrated the ability to adapt and change depending on the conditions and the environment. A leader's frame of mind and health do play a significant role during critical decision-making situations. There is no one apparent leadership trait that determines success, but high energy, integrity, and responsibility make up the fundamental core of a successful leader. Yes, leadership learned, but it also takes the right combination of individual and personality along with cooperative team members to ensure success.

According to Kouzes and Posner, "when operating at their best, leaders: Model the way, inspire a shared vision, challenge the process, enable others to act, and encourage the heart." Successful leaders continually take care of the present while looking ahead and well into the future. The goal of a leader is to ensure the survival of the organization and the individuals under their command. An organization's leadership is responsible for providing the overall strategic planning with a vision towards the future and overall mission accomplishment. Plato once said, "The eyes of the soul of the multitudes are unable to endure the vision of the divine." Historically great leaders have demonstrated an ability to have a different perspective and a comprehensive view of their world. This God-given ability to be able to see things from a different perspective has proven to be the difference between winning and losing or life or death. Great leaders see things with a different eye and are always thinking and processing different scenarios in the minds while thinking and planning the next move like chess masters in the game of life.

According to Gen Omar N. Bradley, Chief of Staff, "Leadership is the art of influencing human behaviour through the ability to influence people and direct them toward a specific goal directly." This definition highlights two fundamental elements: specific goal or task and influencing people to accomplish it. Leaders must be aware of both the task or goal at hand and the people that get it done. Accomplishing the goal should be the primary focus in order to have successful results.

However, a successful leader recognizes that people get things done and need support and guidance to accomplish it. The greatest challenge for a leader is the ability to motivate people; motivating people may be the most challenging part of leadership. Each person has a different personality style with varied learning and development abilities. These individual differences come in the form of intelligence and creativity; each one of us has a different capacity to process information and how we relate to one another. Motivation and attitude determine success; it is an internal state of mind that guides us towards higher achievement and goals.

Successful leaders have specific distinguishing characteristics that separate them from the rest of the pack. Leaders are expected to be honest and truthful, with the right mixture of characteristics and traits. The ability of good leaders making sound decisions is what separates great leaders from their peers while gaining the respect of their followers.

As General George S. Patton famously said, "We herd sheep, we drive cattle, and we lead people. Lead, follow, or get out of the way." It would be safe to say that it is challenging to control or change people around us. Sure, power and authority over them, but this is not real leadership. Authentic leadership is displayed when one turns his back on people, and people will do the right, because they want to, not because of being forced. The most important thing to realize as a leader is to adjust personality to fit the situation and the individuals under command.

According to Hackman and Johnson (2008), leadership shares all the features of human communications. Communication is the lifeline of an organization; it determines how well people interact and work with each other. When lines of communication fail, and organizations struggle and eventually fail to meet their goals or accomplish their mission. The key to successful communications is to realize the importance of identifying various forms of communications and their application to fit the situation or place while applying them skillfully and wisely. Former Air Force Chief of Staff General Thomas D. White believed, "Information is the essential link between wise leadership and purposeful action." Successful leaders listen to what their people have to say and are always looking for good ideas. It is the leader's job to keep all channels of communications open. The more senior a leader becomes the more listening skills they need. Leaders who use words skillfully increase their influence. Leaders need to be aware when they need to be silent and when to speak to truth in order to keep tranquility and peace around there influence of their research and work.

Warren G. Bennis, considered a pioneer in leadership studies, was once asked to describe the difference between leadership and management. He said, "Management is getting people to do what needs. Leadership is getting people to want to do." Leaders must have a grasp of both management and leadership skills in order to maximize their talents and control of their resources. Moreover, leadership and management go hand in hand, and the two should work in harmony. In other words, leadership is an art form in influencing people and management skills are required to run their organization smoothly. The best managers tend to become ethical leaders more because they develop leadership abilities with time and the skills required using proper management techniques. Also, it is seldom that an effective leader is not a good manager; both bring a sense of balance. Successful leaders bring a human touch to management with skills of motivating, influencing, and provide inspirational motivation to anyone they come in meet.

The current work environment is considered a melting pot of different cultures and personalities with self-serving interests at all levels within the organization. Human behaviour influenced by personality styles and external environmental conditions forming from experiences in family, society and the workplace. Organizations have a structured hierarchy of leadership and management, with each level having its own set of values and responsibilities to the chain of command. Its weakest link determines the success of the team. That is why lines of communication and processes not as individual islands but as a collective effort towards the mission or goal.

Hackman and Johnson said: "leadership effectiveness increasingly depends on intercultural emotional competency, the ability to accurately send and receive emotional messages across cultural boundaries." Culture is unique to every organization; it is what defines the group while providing them with a common goal that holds them together towards meeting their objects and goals. The organization leadership should encourage its members to develop shared beliefs and values by creating a culture of trust, optimism, and a system that promotes the idea of continuous improvement in the work environment and leadership and management practices. The climate of the organization points to a shared perception of behaviour rather than beliefs or values. Organizations have distinctive cultures, core values, and beliefs, which provide members with a sense of organizational mission and identity. The success of the organization depends on teamwork; leaders need to create the environment for success; they control the system and have the authority to make changes to the process. In order to satisfy the individual of the organization, management should include them in the decision-making process while encouraging improvement ideas, resulting in better products or outputs for the organization's bottom line or mission.

Leadership is about power, and ethics is about the proper use or misuse of power. The growth or disintegration of the ethical core of each person is the center from which he or she exercises this power. According to Hackman and Johnson, "while power can exist without leadership, leadership cannot exist without power." The six aspects of the power of office are inspirational, charismatic, expert, persuasive, knowledge, and coercive power. Leaders have legitimate power vested on them by legal and formal positions. Referent power is another form of power when the leader over identifies with his people under their command. Expert power, for example, is obtained by individuals with specialized knowledge or skills and these experts play a critical role in running an organization. Coercive power is also a form of unethical power that is sometimes used to punish or maintain control using harmful and manipulative strategies. Power and influence go hand in hand, while good leaders choose the path of righteousness. The key to be an active, ethical leader is to place faith in the forefront while being able to adjust to using the appropriate level of authority required to fit the situation or the task at hand.

Team dynamics include complex interactions between team members while influencing their behaviour and performance. Many forces affect teams; to include different personality styles and types, friendships, relationships, equipment, facilities la.t and design, external influences, senior leaders and managers, and many more. The success of the team will be determined by how well the team will be able to manage and overcome many issues that are part of team dynamics. Stephen Covey's book called Seven Habits of Highly Effective People defines synergy as "The whole is greater than the sum of the parts." All successful individuals and teams realize the importance of synergy. Teams that do not develop synergy have a difficult time accomplishing their goals and tasks, while struggling to coexist with each other. The question is, are team members working well together and supporting each other? If they are not, their chances of success diminish, and on the other hand, if they are jelling and clicking like seconds on a clock, then their chances of success are very likely.

Knowing strengths and weaknesses is critical to effective leadership. The leader must be able to recognize their capabilities and limitations. Former Chief Master Sergeant of the Air Force Robert D. Gaylor put it this way: "Sure, everyone wants to be an effective leader, whether it is in the Air Force or the community. Can and will be if identify strengths, capitalize on them, and consciously strive to reduce and minimize the times apply style inappropriately." Great leaders see things overall and big-picture view while always thinking and planning the next move like chess masters in the game of life. Leadership requires understanding and the willingness to have the right state of mind and a positive attitude. Great leaders rely on wisdom and always try not to repeat the failures of the past while staying on the path of righteousness.

It is easy to conclude that it is challenging for leaders to control or change people around them. Sure, they can use their position power to direct people under their command, but this is real leadership. Leadership is when. Turn back and are not around people will do the right thing because they want to not because told them. The most important thing to realize as a leader is to adjust yourself and personality to fit the situation and the individual, and this is truly effective leadership.

Not sure if can teach leadership, but successful leaders realize the need for change, with continuous adjustments in leadership style to fit the situation. General Patton once said, "on parade every day," meaning that superiors and subordinates watch every move. Make. Character is something. gain from an early age and influenced by family, friends, and society, and it is part of personality. Most of us are born with a sound mind, and we intrinsically know from right and wrong, when. Look more profound, and it comes down to making the right choices. Leadership and character go together, and you will know what you are made of, especially when you are faced with difficult situations while making hard decisions. Will you choose the route of least resistance, or will make the right decision based on a strong character based on traits of integrity, honesty, and courage?

Notes:

Leadership Challenge

Kouzes and Posner (2008), in their book The Leadership Challenge, ask a question if leadership learned? An individual's personality formed by approximately the age of seven and each person has a different personality profile with varied learning and development abilities. These individual differences come in the form of intelligence and creativity; everyone has a different capacity to process information and how he/she relates to the environment and others. Do the old-age questions remain if leaders are born or made? Individuals in any position of authority need to have a breadth of and experience in the areas of leadership and management coupled with the ability to use various psychological profiling techniques in order to be the best leaders they can be. Successful leaders have demonstrated the ability to adapt and change depending on the conditions and the environment. A leader's frame of mind and health do play a significant role during critical decision-making situations. There is no one apparent leadership trait that determines success, but high energy, integrity, and responsibility make up the fundamental core of a successful leader.

According to Kouzes and Posner (2008), "when operating at their best, leaders: Model the way, inspire a shared vision, challenge the process, enable others to act, and encourage the heart." Successful leaders continually take care of the present while looking ahead and well into the future. The goal of a leader is to ensure the survival of the organization and the individuals under their command. An organization's leadership is responsible for providing the overall strategic planning with a vision towards the future and overall mission accomplishment. Plato once said, "The eyes of the soul of the multitudes are unable to endure the vision of the divine." Historically great leaders have demonstrated an ability to have a different perspective and a comprehensive view of their world. This God-given ability to be able to see things from a different perspective has proven to be the difference between winning and losing or life or death. Great leaders see things with a different eye and are always thinking and processing different scenarios in the minds while thinking and planning the next move like chess masters in the game of life.

Warren G. Bennis, considered a pioneer in leadership studies, was once asked to describe the difference between leadership and management. He said, "Management is getting people to do what needs to do. Leadership is getting people to want to do what needs to do." Leaders must have a grasp of both management and leadership skills in order to maximize their talents and control of their resources. Moreover, leadership and management go hand in hand, and the two should work in harmony. In other words, leadership is an art form in influencing people and management skills are required to run their organization smoothly. The best managers tend to become ethical leaders more because they develop leadership abilities with time and the skills required using proper management techniques. Also, it is seldom that an effective leader is not a good manager; both bring a sense of balance. Successful leaders bring a human touch to management with skills of motivating, influencing, and provide inspiration and motivation to people.

According to Gen Omar N. Bradley, Chief of Staff, "Leadership is the art of influencing human behaviour through the ability to influence people and direct them toward a specific goal directly." This definition highlights two fundamental elements: specific goal or task and influencing people to accomplish it. Leaders must be aware of both the task or goal at hand and the people that get it done. Accomplishing the goal should be the primary focus in order to have successful results. However, a successful leader recognizes that people get things done and need support and guidance to accomplish it. The greatest challenge for a leader is the ability to motivate people; motivating people may be the most challenging part of leadership. Each person has a different personality style with varied learning and development abilities. These individual differences come in the form of intelligence and creativity; each one of us has a different capacity to process information and how we relate to one another. Motivation and attitude determine success; it is an internal state of mind that guides us towards higher achievement and goals.

The current work environment is considered a melting pot of different cultures and personalities with self-serving interests at all levels within the organization. Human behaviour influenced by personality styles and external environmental conditions forming from experiences in family, society and the workplace. Organizations have a structured hierarchy of leadership and management, with each level having its own set of values and responsibilities to the chain of command. Its weakest link determines the success of the team. That is why lines of communication and processes learned of not as individual islands but as a collective effort towards the mission or goal.

Culture is unique to every organization; it is what defines the group while providing them with a common goal that holds them together towards meeting their objects and goals. The organization leadership should encourage its members to develop shared beliefs and values by creating a culture of trust, optimism, and a system that promotes the idea of continuous improvement in the work environment and leadership and management practices. The climate of the organization points to a shared perception of behaviour rather than beliefs or values. The organizational climate, on the other hand, consists of internal behavioral characteristics that distinguish one group from another and plays a significant role in influencing the behaviour of the individuals. The climate of the organization can be described by the openness, health, and citizenship between the interactions of the individuals within all levels of the organization. Organizations have distinctive cultures, core values, and beliefs, which provide members with a sense of organizational mission and identity. The success of the organization depends on teamwork; leaders need to create the environment for success; they control the system and have the authority to make changes to the process. In order to satisfy the individual of the organization, management should include them in the decision-making process while encouraging improvement ideas, resulting in better products or outputs for the organization's bottom line or mission.

Successful leaders have specific distinguishing characteristics that separate them from the rest of the pack. Leaders are expected to be honest and truthful, with the right mixture of characteristics and traits. The proverbs teach us first about how to lead our own lives and then the way we should lead others. The ability of good leaders making sound decisions is what separates great leaders from their peers while gaining the respect of their followers. As General George S. Patton famously said, "We herd sheep, we herd cattle, we drive cattle, and we lead people. Lead, follow, or get out of the way." It would be safe to say that it is challenging to control or change people around us. Sure, they can use power and authority over them, but this is not authentic leadership. Leadership is displayed when one turns back on people, and people will do the right thing because they want to, not because told. The most important thing to realize as a leader is to adjust personality to fit the situation and the individuals under command.

Is character learned, or one demonstrates character by example? Successful leaders lead by example, and for example, General Patton once said, "are on parade every day" the people under command will observe every move and action taken; therefore, it is essential to be the best example that can be. Character is something gained from an early age and influenced by family, friends, society, and personality. Most of us are born with a sound mind, and we intrinsically know from right and wrong, when. Look at it comes down to making a choice. Character comes to play, especially when are faced with making hard decisions. Will choose the route of least resistance will make the right decision based on a strong character based on leadership traits of high integrity, honesty, and courage.

Plato once said, "The eyes of the soul of the multitudes are unable to endure the vision of the divine." Successful leaders continually need to seek the truth while gaining knowledge daily in order to secure and create an environment of a spiritual and rewarding experience for the people they lead, now and well into the future. Leader provides the overall strategic planning for the school while promoting cooperation and teamwork with a vision towards mission accomplishment.

The phenomenon of al leadership is about power, and ethics is about the proper use or misuse of power. The growth or disintegration of the ethical fiber of each person is the center from which he or she exercises this power. The six aspects of the power of office are inspirational, charismatic, expert, persuasive, knowledge, and coercive power." Leaders have legitimate power vested on them by district and state agencies. Referent power is another form of power when the leader over identifies with his people under their command. Expert power, for example, is obtained by individuals with specialized knowledge or skills and these experts play a critical role in running an organization. Coercive power is also a form of unethical power that is sometimes used to punish or maintain control using harmful and manipulative strategies. Power and influence go hand in hand, while good leaders choose the path of righteousness.

Successful leaders have specific distinguishing characteristics that separate them from the rest of the pack. Leaders are expected to be honest and truthful, with the right mixture of characteristics and traits. The proverbs teach us first about how to lead our own lives and then the way we should lead others. The ability of good leaders making sound decisions is what separates great leaders from their peers while gaining the respect of their followers. As General George S. Patton famously said, "We herd sheep, we herd cattle, we drive cattle, and we lead people. Lead, follow, or get out of the way." It would be safe to say that it is challenging to control or change people around us. Sure, they can use your power and authority over them, but this is not real leadership. Authentic leadership is displayed when you turn back on people, and people will do the right thing because they want to, not because they told to. The most important thing to realize as a leader is to adjust yourself and personality to fit the situation and the individuals under your command.

Integrity is a total commitment to the highest personal characteristics and professionalism with ethical standards. Leaders must first be honest and truthful in everything they do. Integrity means to establish a set of personal values and not compromising the position or the people under their command. Former Air Force Chief of Staff General Charles Gabriel said, "Integrity is the fundamental premise of military service in a free society. Without integrity, the moral pillars of our military strength, public trust, and self-respect lost." Proverbs teach the fundamental guiding principles of leadership, emphasizing the importance of integrity and value. Great leaders seem to be above reproach and an unwilling will to be compromised and the ability to stay true to their values. What separates leaders, good leaders know the importance of integrity, and without it, they stand to lose the respect of their followers and superiors.

A willingness to act is what good leaders must do; they must have the self-confidence to make timely decisions. The leader must then effectively communicate the decision to their people. British Admiral Sir Roger Keyes emphasized that "In all operations, a moment arrives when brave decisions have made if an enterprise is to be carried through." Of course, decisiveness includes the willingness to accept responsibility. Leaders are always accountable--when things go right and when things go wrong. The law of navigation teaches us to check the source of wisdom and motives while checking the outcomes. Leader provides the overall strategic planning for the school while promoting cooperation and teamwork with a vision towards mission accomplishment.

Knowing strengths and weaknesses is critical to effective leadership. The leader must be able to recognize their capabilities and limitations. Former Chief Master Sergeant of the Air Force Robert D. Gaylor put it this way: "Sure, everyone wants to be an effective leader, whether it is in the Air Force or in the community can and will be if identify strengths, capitalize on them, and consciously strive to reduce and minimize the times apply style inappropriately."

Based on my personnel military experience in leadership and management, it has made me conclude that it is challenging to control or change people around us. Leaders need to be highly ethical individuals with higher standards of integrity and moral values. Leaders in a position of authority that has lasting effects for the people they lead. It is essential for leaders to look at God's example and not to abuse their authority and always stay humble to their approach when dealing with the people under them.

Can leadership be taught?

Our answer is an unequivocal "yes." Isn't it amazing we have never asked the question, "Can management be learned?" We just assumed people could be educated and trained to be managers and further developed into even better managers. Based on this belief, billions of dollars invested in undergraduate and graduate programs. Imagine what might be possible if everyone assumed the same about leadership. Leadership is not just about leaders. Nor is leadership about some position or place in an organization or community. In today's world of unrelenting changes in technology, marketplaces, organizational alliances, mergers, and partnerships; of increasing global competitiveness; of accelerating diversity of ideas along with a rainbow coalition of individual backgrounds, beliefs, abilities, and experiences; of continuing reengineering of processes and right-sizing of organizations and flattening of organizational forms, leadership must be everyone's business.

The caliber of managers raised by assuming people can learn skills and knowledge associated with good management practice. The same can with leadership. Viewing leadership as a non-learnable set of character traits dooms societies, and their organizations, to having only a few good leaders. It is far healthier and more productive to start with the assumption that everyone can lead. We believe in a self-fulfilling prophecy. Once we assume that leadership is learnable, we discover how many good leaders there really are. People do tend to perform to the level of their own and other people's expectations, and this phenomenon documented across adults in the workplace and people in school. If we, as leaders (or parents, or managers, or friends), begin with the assumption that some people have leadership skills and some people do not, then we are likely to get precisely the kind of leaders we expect.

Indeed, we should not mislead people into believing they can attain unrealistic goals. Neither should we assume only a few will ever attain excellence in leadership or any other human endeavor. Those who are most successful at bringing out the best in others are those who set achievable but stretching goals and believe they can develop the talents of others must believe that leadership learned.

We would not have written this leadership challenge if we did not believe ordinary people can learn how to get extraordinary things done. We would not have bothered unless we believed ordinary people could become extraordinary leaders. Chances are you also believe leadership is learned or would not be a leader. Maybe the qualities of leadership will be exhibited on behalf of the organization, or the church, or the community, or the scouts, or the union, or the corporation, or the family. Many have had a leadership story to tell, somewhere, sometime, the leader within each of us gets the call to step forward and do right.

Harry Levinson and Stuart Rosenthal, both psychiatric experts, make this comment about the development of leaders: "Our point of view is that some people want to be leaders and see themselves as leaders. Others rise to the occasion. In either case, they see what must be done and do it. They provide stability and support while defining goals and providing reassurance. Sometimes they become leaders when they become angry about something, catch fire, and start to lead People to become leaders when they learn to take a stand, to take risks, to anticipate, initiate, and innovate."

The same for the leaders we studied. Many of them did not initiate the personal best leadership projects they wrote and talked about, yet they rose to the occasion. Others accepted an assignment and then found drive and change in attitude towards mission accomplishment. None of us may know our real strength until challenged to bring it forth. As an author and social activist Rita Mae Brown has noted: "People are like tea bags" never know how strong they will be until putting into hot water."

What exactly is leadership?

There are over 225 definitions of leadership found in the literature. Pick one! Of course, we offer what works best for us in our work with people (and with managers, government officials, community organizers, health care providers, and al administrators), but we do not claim the last word on "defining" leadership. It has said, "cannot capture a river in a bucket," and we believe the same can told about trying to define leadership. We can investigate, analyze, and examine leadership, but in this endeavor, we too often fail to capture its true essence.

Historian Arthur M. Schlesinger, Jr. has pointed out: "The very concept of leadership implies the proposition that individuals make a difference to history." This point of ordinary people at their personal best as leaders. When Philip L. Smith, as president and chief operating officer of General Foods, discussed leadership with groups of senior managers in the company's executive development program, he asked each to "share a story about a leader or leaders who have had a profound impact upon his or her life and values." As a result of this free and open exchange, he reported that participants get a strong message: "Just as leaders have influenced them, so too can they have a lasting and compelling impact on the people they manage."

Virtually all of us can name at least one leader whose compelling impact we have felt. Sometimes it is a well-known figure out of the past that changed the course of history. Sometimes we choose contemporary role models who served as examples of success. Still, others are those who helped us learn coaches, leaders, parents, friends, managers. Leaders make a difference, and that is why we care so much about the development of leadership, especially among organizations. In a series of studies involving work environments leaders (summarized later), leadership within organizational effectiveness.

We believe that leadership is a set of skills. Like any skill, with the proper motivation and desire, with practice and feedback, through role models and coaching, this skill can be strengthened, honed, and enhanced. The set of skills articulated in The Leadership Challenge does not explain 100 per cent of the variance when it comes to leadership—but what social science model does? We explain a substantial (and statistically significant) amount of the variance, and our framework is a relatively simple and understandable place to start learning about being a leader. This framework has proved quite useful and robust across a variety of disciplines not only for teaching about leadership but in helping people acquire and develop their leadership skills.

How does one become the kind of person who makes a difference? How do we teach people to become the best leaders possible? In our studies, as well as others by the Center for Creative Leadership and corporations like Honeywell, three significant opportunities for learning to emerge: (a) trial and error, (b) observation of others, and (c) formal and training will see these three elements prominently incorporated in the course designs that follow. Some instructors have built their course specifically upon The Leadership Challenge, and others have included it as one of many other resources in their course design.

According to Kouzes and Posner (2008), "when operating at their best, leaders: Model the way, inspire a shared vision, challenge the process, enable others to act, and encourage the heart."

The Five Practices, more frequently than do at present, will be more effective. We know from our research that those who Model, Inspire, Challenge, Enable, and Encourage more frequently are more likely to get extraordinary things done than those who do so less frequently. Exemplary leadership, in other words, is not an accident of birth or circumstance. It is a result of conscious and conscientious practice. To model effectively, must first believe in something. As a leader, are supposed to stand up for beliefs, so. It is better to have some beliefs to stand up for. The first commitment must make, then, is to find a voice by clarifying values and then expressing them in an authentically own style.

Leaders envision the future. They gaze across the horizon of time, imagining the attractive opportunities that are in store once they and their constituents arrive at the destination. Leaders have a desire to make something happen, to change how things are, to create something that no one else has ever created before.

Leaders are pioneers' people who are willing to step out into the unknown. They search for opportunities to innovate, grow, and improve. Nevertheless, no leader can be the only creator or originator of new products, services, or processes. Product and service innovations tend to come from customers, clients, vendors, people in the labs, and people on the front lines, while process innovations tend to come from the people making the work primary contribution to the search for opportunities is in recognition of good ideas, the support of those ideas, and the willingness to challenge the system in order to get new products, processes, services, and systems adopted. Leaders know well that innovation and change require them to experiment and take risks. One way of dealing with the potential risks and failures of experimentation is to approach change through incremental steps and small wins. Little victories, when piled on top of each other, build enough confidence to meet even the most significant challenges. By incrementally strengthen the commitment to the long-term future. Nevertheless, not everyone is equally comfortable with risk and uncertainty also must pay attention to the capacity of constituents to take control of challenging situations and become fully committed to change.

Exemplary leaders enable others to Act. They foster collaboration and build trust. This sense of teamwork goes far beyond a few direct reports or close confidants. In today's "virtual" organization, cooperation restricted to a small group of loyalists; it must include peers, managers, customers and clients, suppliers, citizens, all those who have a stake in the vision have to involve, in some way, everyone who must live with the results and must make it possible for others to do good work.

Encouragement can come from dramatic gestures or simple actions. It is part of the leader's job to recognize contributions by showing appreciation for individual excellence. In the cases we collected, there were thousands of examples of individual recognition. We have heard and seen everything, including marching bands, costumed skits, "This Is Life" imitations, as well as

The Five Practices and Ten Commitments of Exemplary Leadership

Model the Way

Find Voice by clarifying values.

Set the example by aligning actions with shared values.

Inspire a Shared Vision

Envision the future by imagining exciting and ennobling possibilities.

Enlist others in a common vision by appealing to shared aspirations.

Challenge the Process

Search for opportunities by seeking innovative ways to change, grow, and improve.

Experiment and take risks by constantly generating small wins and learning from mistakes.

Enable others to act

Foster collaboration by promoting cooperative goals and building trust.

Strengthen others by sharing power and discretion.

Encourage the heart

Recognize contributions by showing appreciation for individual excellence.

Celebrate the values and victories by creating a spirit of community.

LEADERSHIP IS EVERYONE'S BUSINESS

The next time say, "Why don't they do something about that?" look in the mirror. Ask the person to see, "Why do not do something about that?" By accepting the challenge to lead comes to realize that the only limits are those places. We need more leaders today, not fewer. We need more people to accept responsibility for bringing about significant changes in what we do and how we do it. We need more people to answer the call. The world needs talents.

The best leaders are continually learning. They see all experiences as learning experiences. Nevertheless, there is a catch. Unexamined experiences do not produce rich insights that come from reflection and analysis. To become a better leader, we need to study their performance and become more conscious about the choices that. are making and how they are acting on your intentions.

To inspire a shared vision for the future by imagining exciting and ennobling possibilities and enlist others in the dreams by appealing to shared aspirations. To Challenge the Process, search for opportunities by seeking innovative ways to change, grow, and improve, and experiment and take risks by constantly generating small wins and learning from mistakes. To Enable Others to Act, Foster collaboration by promoting cooperative goals and building trust, and strengthen others by sharing power and discretion. Leadership is a relationship and a good relationship with trust. Trust is fostered by listening and attending to the other person.

To encourage the heart, recognize contributions by showing appreciation for individual excellence, and Celebrate the values and victories by creating a spirit of community. Recognizing individual contributions to the values and the achievements of the project are an opportunity not only to Encourage the Heart of team members but also to reinforce your project values. Every project milestone is an opportunity for team members to celebrate what they have accomplished and gather spirit and momentum to continue. Public ceremonies serve another compelling purpose. They bring people closer together. As we move to a more virtual world where communication is by voice mail, e-mail, cell phone, videoconference, and pager, it is becoming more and more difficult for people to find opportunities to be together. We are social animals, and we need each other — those who are fortunate enough to have lots of social support. Social support is essential to our well-being and productivity. Celebrating together is one way we can get that essential support.

Notes:

Principles of Leadership

ccording to Maxwell, "Leaders need to respond to individuals based on their needs rather than their faults. Proverbs 25-21-22 encourages us to see what others need, even our enemies, and respond accordingly." Individuals in any position of authority need to have a breadth of and experience in dealing with all types of people. God has given us all an individual conscience and different personality; good leaders realize this and adapt their leadership style based on the needs of each personality and the situation. Leaders, for example, may want to incorporate a more direct teaching approach with your people. While in the higher levels, a leader may be wise to use a lazier fair or participative style of leadership in order to accommodate the more advanced people.

Good leaders not only adopt and apply situational leadership principles but as stated in Proverbs 23 good leaders also have a vision by planning towards the future. Leaders must be of high ethical standards of character and principles; they must have a high moral character with a vision towards the future. Leaders affect the lives of many people, and they must be big-picture thinkers while leading with a visionary view. They must continually seek the truth and gain knowledge daily in order to create an environment of a spiritual and rewarding experience for the people they lead well into the future.

Proverbs 22:6 provides valuable lessons for parents on how to be kind and just leaders for their people. Leaders play a crucial role in the development of subordinates, and it all starts with building character and by providing proper discipline. An individual that has not been taught the fundamental basics of good character and disciplined at an early part of their lives will more than likely have deficiencies in these areas into more responsibilities. Discipline is the core building block of creating individuals with high integrity and moral values. Without discipline, everything is lost, especially in people; they need a structured upbringing that includes encouragement and positive role models.

Proverbs teach the fundamental guiding principles of leadership, emphasizing the importance of values, character, and wisdom of a leader.

Leaders seem to be big-picture thinkers, and this ability of a complete mental view is what may separate them from their followers. The scriptures teach that every one of us can be a good leader; by having a strong will to succeed and attitude to strive to improve and seek wisdom continuously, excellent leadership skills achieved. The Book of Proverbs is all about; it is a road map for individuals to improve their thinking process and to build strong moral values based on God's teachings. The proverbs teach us first about how to lead our own lives and then the way we should lead others. The ability of good leaders making sound decisions is what separates great leaders from their peers while gaining the respect of their followers.

King Solomon issues a warning concerning a leader's authority and character, "When leaders try to exercise authority without a servant's heart, they eventually hurt themselves. Leaders add value by serving others" Ecclesiastes 8:1-9. Leaders need to be individuals of strong character and faith while putting God and people first above their ambitions and interests. Leaders should strive to keep safely in their hearts and soul their servitude to the higher authority of God.

Leaders must not be conceited and vein because "The Lord giveth and the Lord taketh away" (Job 1:21). Leaders can lead without leading and by being silent and positive role models while at the same time, realizing their limitations and recognizing the higher order of God's master plan. According to Proverbs on ants and leadership, "Ants do not need a leader to tell them to get started. Ants work faithfully and need no outside accountability to keep them doing right. Ants work hard and will replace their anthill when it gets ruined" Proverbs 6:6-8.

Leaders need to allow people to be able to use their creativity and freedom of expression for them to grow spiritually and academically. God has given us the tiniest creature to learn from, individuals striving to be leaders can learn much from the ants. The first lesson is that individuals should have the authority and flexibility to oversee their affairs. This character trait was probably most active, by allowing subordinates to take charge of their tasks or missions gave them a sense of empowerment and self-responsibility. The role changed from an authoritarian figure to a facilitator and leader. The personnel leadership weakness would believe most individuals want to do a good job; many times, it is the leader that fails his people, and this occurs because they do not provide them with the proper training and guidance while placing unnecessary limitations on them. Leaders influence people by leading by example, must get out behind the desk, and be in the front lines with your people for them to respect and look.

Leaders would be wise to develop quality measures throughout the entire process, ensuring people develop progressively and continuously. If quality built into the system at the front end, there would be no need to test at the back end. Using standards of higher moral and ethical characteristics rooted in the teachings of the scriptures will ensure people a well-rounded based on a more significant religious order. In an al system designed around trust, ethical standards, and high moral character, people would likely take more responsibility for their learning. The scriptures provide a wealth of knowledge and wisdom for people and will only enrich their lives if they seek its fountain of truth and knowledge. Faith gives individuals personnel balance while enriching their spirit with wholesome Godly goodness.

According to Proverbs in the section of the Irony of Spiritual Leaders, "Godly leaders think without lines: They let God outside of the box." The Proverbs mention that even sound wisdom separated from God can become an obstacle for individuals. The Proverbs describe that God should be allowed outside these boundaries of decision making. By allowing people to include faith as a big part of there, it would provide people with the opportunity to be better prepared for spiritual growth while at the same time providing answers that science cannot answer.

The scriptures give people hop and self-intuition based on a higher order of spiritual thinking process. Jeffersonian al ideals of open universities may be the out of the box thinking in today's system. The open school system will allow people to take classes as needed with no restrictions. The open school system would place more emphasis on experimentation and less on memorizing while allowing people freedom of expression to develop spiritually and grow intellectually.

Notes:

Case Study: Twelve O'clock High

T welve O'clock High, the 1949 war movie about American aircrews flying missions over Nazi Germany during World War II. Colonel Keith Davenport (Gary Merrill) was the commander of the massive bombardment group stationed in England during the early days of the war. Davenport was very popular amongst his men, but his group suffered in discipline and heavy aircraft losses, gaining the reputation as the "hard luck group". He was considered one of the boys and was very close to his men, and they, in turn, liked him for his casual style of leadership. He understood the dangers of placing his men at arm's length from the fight and this made him question many orders from higher headquarters. Major General Patrick Pritchard (Millard Mitchell), commanding general visited the group and realized the reason for the high loses and poor discipline was due in part to Davenport's over-identification to his men, contributing to his inability to lead. Pritchard orders a change of command and asks Brigadier General Frank Savage (Gregory Peck) to take over the job.

When General Savage arrives at his new command, he finds everything in disarray and begins making changes to correct these problems. He implements harsh disciplinary actions throughout the group, and the men immediately wished Davenport was back and start to dislike him. He is particularly hard on executive officer Lieutenant Colonel Ben Gately (Hugh Marlowe) and places him under arrest for being absent without leave. Many of the pilots asked to transfer from the group in order to get away from his command. Savage through his secretary, stalls the airmen from completing their transfer application in order to buy more time. After Savage leads the group on a few successful bombing missions, returning all the aircraft to base, the airmen begin to change their minds of their new commander. The pilots eventually realize that Savage was looking out for their interest and had to implement an authoritarian style of leadership for them to be a disciplined group of fighters, contributing to the success of their mission while saving many of the pilot's lives in the process. General Savage is transformed from an authoritarian style leader at first then to a participative leader that included his pilots on the decision-making processes to finally breaking down from exhaustion and the sight of losing several of his top pilots.

Should Pete Marshall transfer?

Colonel Davenport, in many ways, represents the older leader. They are both very popular with their people and managed in a similar lazier fair style of leadership. Now, the new leader is in the same position as General Savage taking over command of the flight group or school in disarray. Savage immediately implemented harsh disciplinary actions and even placing some members in jail in order to restore control and command. New leaders can learn a few lessons from General Savage and should implement measures to restore order and discipline throughout his school. The first step should be to meet with all his staff and leaders on one to one basis to find out about the people under his command. The next step should include speaking to his entire group and inform them of the institutions operating regulations and rules; to include each and everyone's responsibility and duties. The leader should start enforcing the rules and regulations of the organization in order to restore credibility to his office. In many instances, he should start handing out letters of admonishment to individuals that break or not follow the rules and regulations of the school.

Leaders can implement many different forms of management and leadership styles to run their organization. Most of the time, a leader must lead from the center or situational leadership style and to adapt to the situation at hand. In this situation, many of his staff and leaders are resistant to the change of leadership, and they are rebelling in their way in a similar situation to General Savage when he had to deal with his pilot's resentment against him. The question asks if he should transfer. No, he should be able to stay, and he does have many years of experience and is well-liked by his peers and can serve the new leader in many ways. General Sung Tzu once said, "keep friends close and enemies even closer." The new principle should keep him closer to him and have a come to Jesus talk to hash out any differences. Within time the staff and leaders will learn to work better and respect the new leader after the storm settles.

Supportive secretary?

Again, the new leader should have a one-on-one counselling session to discuss the responsibilities of their position and any other issues as required. Besides, the new principle should make precise requirements and the importance of having the full cooperation and support from staff. If the secretary continues to demonstrate deficient performance and disobey orders, the leader should quickly start admonishment procedures to correct the harmful behaviour. These are harsh leadership techniques, especially for people that have been in these positions for many years and only should be used as a last option to restore control and command. People, by nature, resist change, and one method of changing these behaviours is to think of the process over time and a process like melting an ice cube. The ice cube starts as a frozen block in similar fashion people have habits formed like a block of ice. For change to occur, the ice cube has melted to water; in addition, an individual provides new processes, and over time, be allowed to change, and once the individual learns new habits, he forms them back to the refrozen ice cube.

Authority for change?

There are two types of authority, earned and position power. A leader strives to earn his respect from his people and only uses his position power to establish law and order. The new leader should re-establish command and control while enforcing the rules and regulations of the school. The key is for the new principle is to establish a report with his staff and his leaders through open communication and dialogue.

Top-down changes?

There is no need to make additional changes now; making drastic changes to staff and leaders could disrupt the flow of that could trickle down to the people. In time, it may make sense to provide staff and leaders opportunities to rotate within the organization or to a different organization. Many people do get bored with their work and transferring, or rotating people does provide them with a new outlook and a chance to get invigorated. It seems that the staff and leaders do have a good working relationship established already, and they need to give positive encouragement for their efforts and at the same time, informed of their responsibilities to the people and the school.

Rules, regulations, and procedures?

Organizations already have rules and regulations; the problem seems the enforcement of those rules. The new principle must conduct himself professionally and to treat everyone fairly and respectfully while being careful not to show favoritism. The new leader should review the rules and regulations and implement changes if required with the consensus of upper management and staff.

Is it time for dramatic restructuring?

The organization should be intact because they are dealing with a professional group of leaders and administrators that have many years' experience. They enjoyed their autonomy and got lax with many of the rules because they were led with minimum supervision; by no means, this is an excellent excuse to break regulations, and they may have taken advantage of in many ways. The new leader must reverse this trend and habits while instilling order and discipline back to the organization at all levels.

Participative, an unrealistic dream?

For starter, the old leader is not here anymore, and there is a new leader. Authoritarian leadership style is more important currently to quickly pull the reins and establish order and discipline throughout the organization. As things settle, it is much better to rule from the center and provide positive and encouraging to the staff and employees in order to facilitate high moral. A happy leader reflects his mood to his people.

Notes:

What Good Institutions Do

T his article emphasizes the importance of character and the traits significant linked to leadership that includes selflessness, decisiveness, energy, commitment, loyalty, and integrity. Good leaders have these personality characteristics of emotional stability, enthusiasm, conscientiousness, tough-mindedness, and self-assurance based on a foundation of faith. The author also discusses the importance of developing programs to teach character in the classroom. Also, it describes different initiatives taken from several institutions and programs involving community service and other group activities. Strong moral character is what followers expect and look for in a good leader. Character is something gain from an early age, influenced by family, friends, and environmental conditions.

Most of us are born with a sound mind, and we intrinsically know from right and wrong; when Look at it comes down to making the right conscience choice. It is reasonable to assume that character and personality traits are associated with leadership, while others are not. Many times, we focus on character and leadership traits associated with success, but it is interesting to understand failures of leadership as well. Some leaders forget about the goal and concentrate on themselves instead of the whole. Negative characteristic traits that can affect leadership consist of selfishness, meaning that we concentrate on our needs and not the good of others. As a leader, will choose the route of least resistance or will the right decision based on traits of integrity, honesty, and courage in sync with the teachings of the scriptures?

Notes:

Professional Integrity

If leadership described with one word, it would be "Professional" to be a professional. Must be committed towards the betterment of society overall. Professional fully describes an al leader, because most leaders serve most of their adult life in their positions serving others. Leaders considered professionals through their actions, as demonstrated by self-sacrifice, devotion, and passion towards and their subordinate's well-being.

Leaders must possess the highest ethical standards and personal characteristics in order to be effective in their day-to-day activities. Professional leadership traits consist of integrity, loyalty, honesty, and a commitment to mission accomplishment. Integrity means to be above reproach with an unwavering character to stay true to the cause. Character-based on high ethical standards is what makes an al leader respected by their superiors, peers, community, and their people. Leaders are entrusted and serve as role models for their people. Responsibility to raise people right not only falls on the shoulders of leaders but to community leaders and they all must be active partners towards success of their people.

During a group think tank exercise, our group consisted of individuals with varied and professional backgrounds; the one thing that stands out about team members is the character. They all had a sense of professionalism about them, along with leadership traits based on high moral character, integrity, and honesty — these same leadership traits displayed during the entire process of completing the group assignment and presentation. The smooth and cooperative efforts of all team members were evident; no one team member was overbearing or had to have it his or her way and this led towards synergy within the group. The first step of the team decision-making process was the planning stage; on the first day we discussed the entire case study and investigated the organization's strategic plans and the working environment and the community. The second step was to identify the root problems and offer several solutions. The third step was to agree upon two criteria and provide detailed plans for implementation. The final step was to present our findings and allow for open debate and discussion. Our team plan provided a road map towards securing the work environment while emphasizing retaining qualified leaders.

Professionals serving in any capacity have an obligation towards seeking further and continuously improving in the way they lead and manage their day-to-day activities and their lives. Based on experience, the most impact and to the way I view and see the world around me would be the experience, and I gained while serving in the U.S. Air Force for over 20 years of active duty. Dr. W. Edwards Deming, with his philosophy on life in general, along with his famous Total Quality Management (14 Point) theories, provide a leader with a rich foundation based on a never-ending cyclical process of continues improvement. The second most important tool a good leader should possess is the ability to read people using various personality profiling techniques in their jobs and their lives.

Understanding your people and being aware of one's capabilities and limitations may determine the success or failure of a leader in many circumstances. Leaders should attend professional conferences and seminars if time and funds are available. With today's financial constraints, many organizations are turning towards online seminars and training programs to save funds and time.

Along with training seminars, there are many self-improvement books and magazines that are specific and may fit in the overall scheme of improving the leadership and management capabilities of an al leader. The World Wide Web is a rich source of information that provides an overabundance of information and the capability to join social and professional organizations online. Today al leaders have access to many resources to share and collaborate with their professional peers exchanging ideas and best practices.

The primary difference between leaders and followers is perspective. The primary difference between leaders is perspective, while both leaders and followers can have a strong character and can possess warm relational skills. Leaders and followers can even have a strong personality and a strong will, and what separates them is how they think and perceive reality. Because the scriptures teach, we are all made to rule, and everyone possesses the capacity to raise their level of leadership abilities. Everyone can improve their leadership skills and the approach they use in influencing others. We must, however, begin with a leadership perspective and that is the main ingredient that makes the Book of Proverbs so profound. Proverbs are about gaining wisdom and continually improving the thinking process and doing things smartly.

A willingness to act is what good leaders must do; they must have the self-confidence to make timely decisions. The leader must then effectively communicate the decision to their people. British Admiral Sir Roger Keyes emphasized that "In all operations, a moment arrives when brave decisions made if an enterprise is to be carried through." Of course, decisiveness includes the willingness to accept responsibility. Leaders are always accountable--when things go right and when things go wrong.

The leader provides the overall strategic planning for the organization while promoting cooperation and teamwork with a vision towards mission accomplishment. The leaders are responsible for creating the framework by which staff and people interact with each other in implementing the goals within their environment. Organizations leaders must promote a positive and nurturing culture that recognizes excellence in the work environment.

Leader provides the overall strategic planning for the school while promoting cooperation and teamwork. Organizational leaders are responsible for creating the framework by which people interact with each other in implementing the goals within their environment. Leaders must promote a positive and nurturing culture that recognizes excellence in teaching and curriculum. Many professions rely on teamwork as an example in the military environment. If the team fails, the mission fails. Individuals in the military are in a situation where they need to contribute to the overall mission by sharing their knowledge and expertise. There are many situations where an individual may have more knowledge about a topic, and they are not willing to share or help their fellow teammates because they feel a sense of power from the knowledge they possess.

Teamwork and sharing of information with one another not only provide a definite feeling of knowing that helped someone, but it also creates a positive environment of sharing and trust that can be used to accomplish the task or mission more effectively and efficiently. We need to look at smarter ways to help people work better together and place less heavy emphasis on inspections and assessments.

According to the Teal Trust (2001) Leadership Style Indicator, "Within pioneering leadership, we consider those who are willing to push themselves and take appropriate risks in striving to move forward to discover and reach long term goals. In a religious context, we can quote Philippians 3: "forgetting what is behind and straining for what lies ahead." Pioneering leaders are passionate about the vision and are wholly committed to it. Paul is an excellent example of a leader focused on pushing out the boundaries of the church, despite personal risk. Pioneering leaders are at their most active in the early stages of a vision or project, excited by seeking out where God is calling. However, as time passes, they may lose interest in the implementation of a vision, eager to be looking ahead to the next challenge."

"Jesus called them together and said, "Know that those who are regarded as rulers of the Gentiles lord it over them, and their high officials exercise authority over them. Not so with. Instead, whoever wants to become great. Must be servant, and whoever wants to be first must be slave of all. For even the Son of Man did not come to be served, but to serve, and to give his life as a ransom for many." Mark 10:42-45. To be good stewards, whoever can be trusted with very little can also be trusted with much, and whoever is dishonest with very little will also be dishonest with much. Luke 16:10.

SOCIAL RESPONSIBILITY

Social responsibility means to be a responsible and respectful individual, demonstrating common courtesy towards others by listening to what they have to say and being silent as they speak. Respect is a two-way street; as a leader, must show respect up and down the chain of command. The social responsibility of a leader should be directly related to the goal and common good of the team. The goal was to create a collaborative and non-confrontational environment between the team. Everyone in the team was professional in every sense of the word.

INTEGRITY

Leadership is about having integrity and a total commitment to the highest personal ethical standards. As a proven leader, feel that actions speak for themselves, and during this course, the main concern was always towards the wellbeing of team members. On many occasions, speak out, but intentions are good, and try to get to the point by being honest and truthful with feedback. Integrity, to a good leader, means to have a backbone and stand up for people under command. Recognize the importance of integrity, and without it, everything lost; respect, loyalty, and commitment.

PROFESSIONALISM

Professionalism characterized by a set of values and characteristics that describe individual actions towards the betterment of society. Professionals are held to a higher set of standards and should contribute their efforts towards the service of others. After serving for over 20 years in the US Air Force may qualify as a professional, placing duty and country above all. Team members were outstanding citizens and professionals that have devoted most of their lives to the betterment of society. Grateful to team members for their commitment and help in completing the final team project.

Maslow's Hierarchy

Maslow's hierarchy of social needs is a theory in psychology proposed by Abraham Maslow in his paper "A Theory of Human Motivation" that involves emotionally based relationships, for example, friendship, intimacy, and supportive family. People need to feel they belong and accepted within their group. Team members need to find ways to work well together and to make each other feel accepted and part of the team. The feeling of acceptance provides confidence building will help them be more successful in accomplishing their goal or task and help in developing well into the future. Maslow's hierarchy of needs determined by order of importance, consisting of a pyramid with five levels. The pyramid starts with the lowest level of physiological needs, while the top-level is associated with self-actualization needs. The higher needs in this hierarchical pyramid only achieved when the lower needs. When the individual moves to the next higher level the lower level will no longer be a priority.

Risk-taking is part of a learning process for a leader; in many instances, a leader must fall in order to learn and develop into a mature and wise leader. Leaders need to be risk-takers while applying different approaches to leading with continuous improvements gained by experience in dealing with all types of individuals and situations. Leaders can apply different leadership styles to stimulate and engage followers to focus on mission goals. Leaders must establish nurturing environments where open debate and calculated risk-taking for process improvement are applauded and not admonished.

They are providing individuals with opportunities to experiment and takes risks to teach valuable lessons, which could potentially produce enormous rewards for the organization and its people. Lessons learned by experimental work and risk-taking have been responsible for most of the societies' advances in technology and medicine and other fields. Individuals best learn by doing and solving problems and share ideas and information with other team members. Brainstorming sessions are one of the tools that can be used to help teams contribute their ideas and theories in order to find the best possible solutions. Everyone within a group motivated in different ways, and it is up to a leader to motive and keep the team focused on the goal. Team members develop a rapport with each other, and the team leader has the responsibility to provide guidance and vision towards the goal while creating an environment of trust, sense of belonging, and purpose.

The organizational climate, on the other hand, consists of internal behavioral characteristics that distinguish one group from another and plays a significant role in influencing the behaviour of the individuals. The climate of the organization can be described by the openness, health, and citizenship between the interactions of the individuals within all levels of the organization. Leaders need to be highly ethical individuals with higher standards of integrity and moral values. Leaders in a position of authority that has lasting effects for the people they lead.

As leaders climb up the ladder of power, so does their abilities to make decisions narrow, with limited options except to choose the path of righteousness or risk it all and fail. Being a good leader means being fair and balanced in decision making while treating people with the utmost respect and dignity. Successful leaders see things before followers do; they see beyond what followers do, and they see bigger than followers do. While followers may barely feel able to see and plan beyond next week, leaders must think, envision, and plan well into the future.

Human civilization has reached the crossroads; machines have taken overproduction in many sectors of manufacturing, surpassing human capability by a thousand-fold. Machines are producing an abundance never witnessed before; with this trend, the human workforce will diminish rapidly shortly. Laws of supply and demand in economics teach, as production goes up, demand goes down, and prices drop; with scarcity, demand goes up, and prices increase.

Manufacturers control the system and can deliberately manipulate the numbers and quality as they see fit. Manufacturers produce inferior products as a scheme to generate continuous income as parts break and need replacement. The problem with our current system is that corporations are concerned with their bottom line and profit margins; this is happening in front of our eyes, all you have to do is look around, and every industry is cutting costs by eliminating human labor and replacing them with machines; for example the automotive industry is almost entirely automated. We are at a stage in human history for a new philosophy a new and different approach in distributing resources required to sustain life and maintain balance in society. The focus on topics concerning the effectiveness of our system and all the players involved in that process. The system challenged like never to be more efficient and productive to meet the demands of the marketplace and future needs. The forces between political, social, and leaders seem to be pulling in all directions; the key is to bring everyone together in creating the best possible system we are trying to help in the first place, our people.

The goal is to examine the relevance of biblical studies in mainstream society further, and politics as they relate to a local and global crisis. The focus is to discover how to implement ancient biblical philosophy into today's new contemporary thinking and ideology of faith as they relate with local and global governments along with the business market. A biblical debate in professional settings provides for the opportunity for intelligent analysis and open debate of the scriptures, offering an interdisciplinary dialogue between biblical scholars, philosophers, and experts.

Human civilization has reached the crossroads; machines have taken overproduction in many sectors of manufacturing, surpassing human capability by a thousand-fold. Technology is responsible for the production of an abundance never witnessed before; with this trend, the human workforce has diminished rapidly, making and historical overview of biblical study can cross over and establish a presence in the decision-making process concerning local and global issues. The integration of scriptures aims to find ways of bridging the gap between relevant Religious philosophy and contemporary thinking and methodology in addressing the crisis in today's global society.

In the last few decades, there has been an increased concern for the establishment of a more sustained interdisciplinary dialogue between biblical scholars and philosophers of many disciplines. As with any movement, and especially establishing a biblical presence in society, will be met with resistance from philosophers, scholars, and political figures to maintain the stronghold of separation between church and state. Whatever the mixed, religious leaders must stay on course in spreading the gospels while demonstrating an appreciation for the fundamental

Religious doctrine and philosophy. It is apparent that world leaders are not capable of finding lasting solutions to the global crisis facing human civilization, the right solutions seem to point towards the Words of God. Will man be capable of diverting the epic biblical catastrophe or continuing the path of a godless world and self-destruction?

Notes:

Art of Leadership, Influence, and Empowerment

Leaders must strive towards more significant personal and professional standards with the highest ethical and moral characteristics. Leaders touch the lives of many, and for this, they must be wise thinkers with a vision towards the future, leading with a worldly view under God's direction. Good leaders demonstrate strong faith in God and always seek His guidance in order to create an environment of a spiritual and rewarding experience for the people they lead. This research paper investigates the characteristics and ethical standards required of all leaders, as related to integrity, loyalty, selflessness, and decisiveness. In addition to stable, ethical characteristics, successful leaders are required to possess the ability to influence, motivate, educate, and build teamwork, all while being an effective communicator. Leaders must challenge themselves in being the best leaders they can be while being positive role models by demonstrating leadership in action based on faith, integrity, and the moral obligation for the betterment of the people under their command.

Vision

Plato once said, "The eyes of the soul of the multitudes are unable to endure the vision of the divine." Successful leaders continually need to seek the truth while gaining knowledge daily in order to secure and create an environment of a spiritual and rewarding experience for the people they lead, now and well into the future. Leader provides the overall strategic planning for the school while promoting cooperation and teamwork with a vision towards mission accomplishment. The law of navigation teaches leaders to integrate wisdom into the motives of decision making for the present with a vision towards the future. The school leaders are responsible for creating the framework by which staff, faculty, and people interact with each other in implementing the goals within their environment. Leaders must promote a positive and nurturing culture that recognizes excellence in mission accomplishment.

Solomon said, "we do not control the timing of most events; the best we can do is to recognize the timing" (Ecclesiastes 3:1-8). The world is continuously moving and changing at a rapid pace; bold initiatives need in order to face the challenges of today and the future. Continuous study and experimentation of the brain is the key to unlock the mystery that will someday provide us with better ideas and methods that need to take in order to maximize our creativity and individuality. The system should stress the importance of science, coupled with the role and balance of faith. We all are born with unlimited potential from the first day of birth; the challenge is to break down barriers and walls society artificially places. God has given us an incredible potential of our brain that can take us anywhere an individual's imagination wants to go. The limits are boundless!

Good leaders not only adapt to the situation, but they also apply different leadership styles to meet their daily tasks or missions. As stated in Proverbs, good leaders always have a plan for today and a vision for tomorrow. Leaders also must be useful planners with a vision towards meeting future needs. Leaders affect the lives of many people and for this reason, must be big-picture thinkers always thinking and planning. While leading requires everyday activities, it is important to plan not only for today but with a visionary view plan for tomorrow.

Influence

Leadership is considered an art of being able to influence and directing people to accomplish the task or mission. Effective leadership hinges on two fundamental concepts; being able to take care of the people, because it takes people to accomplish the task or mission. Spiritual leaders give praise to the higher authority of God, for He is the one that makes everything possible. God provides leaders with the natural ability to influence their people, with wisdom gained through experience and a never-ending quest for the truth. The Proverbs 18:21 say leadership is the law of influence and the evolution of leadership skills. Successful leaders seem to be able to influence the people under their command to go beyond their expected abilities. Successful leaders possess high energy, integrity, and ambition to succeed while showing sincerity and care for the people under their command. Experienced leaders cannot accomplish the mission alone and need the support of their people in order to be successful.

According to Proverbs 10:6-32, "The law of influence must have a skillful tongue. Many verses in Proverbs speak of the tongue and how to use it as a positive influence. Leaders who use words skillfully increase their influence." al leaders need to be aware of when they need to speak and be silent in order to keep tranquility and peace around there people. The law of influence provides leaders with the ability to have a skillful tongue. Good leaders, who develop the use of words skillfully, in turn, increase their ability to influence their followers.

In the words of Proverbs 17:2, "It is better to be a wise slave than a foolish son." Wise leaders realize that power does not come from their position, but the ability to use the rules of empowerment. A significant responsibility of a leader is to groom the people under their command, to be able to step in and take over the project or mission at a moment's notice. In order to fully develop their people, leaders must delegate responsibilities and empower their people to think and act on their own. By empowering people, leaders are, in fact distributing workload and allowing for cooperation while making team members feel that they are an essential and intricate part of the process to complete the overall mission.

Ethics and Power

The phenomenon of al leadership is about power, and ethics is about the proper use or misuse of power. The growth or disintegration of the ethical fiber of each person is the center from which he or she exercises this power. The six aspects of the power of office are inspirational, charismatic, expert, persuasive, knowledge, and coercive power. Leaders have legitimate power vested on them by district and state agencies. Referent power is another form of power when the leader over identifies with his people under their command. Expert power, for example, is obtained by individuals with specialized knowledge or skills and these experts play a critical role in running an organization. Coercive power is also a form of unethical power that is sometimes used to punish or maintain control using harmful and manipulative strategies. Power and influence go hand in hand, while good leaders choose the path of righteousness. Godly leaders remain ethical and use their position to influence people towards the good of the many, while at the same time meeting the goals of the organization. The key to be an active, ethical leader is to place faith in the forefront while being able to adjust to using the appropriate level of authority required to fit the situation or the task at hand.

The Hebrew priests of Sanhedrin drummed up charges, for no acts but of the spoken word of Jesus and accused Him of blasphemy. The priests did not have the authority to place Jesus to death, so they turned to Pontius Pilate. Pilot the Roman governor in Judea found Jesus innocent; stirred priests, he let the citizens choose His fate. While the scriptures teach us to show support for our elected leaders, the question remains what people supposed to do when their elected leaders are unethical and abuse their power are? Proverbs 21:1 says, "Like the rivers of water, He turns it wherever He wishes." Wise and ethical leaders realize that although they are in a position of power, deep inside, they know the differences between being in charge and being out of control.

Notes:

Leadership Characteristics

Successful leaders have specific distinguishing characteristics that separate them from the rest of the pack. Leaders are expected to be honest and truthful, with the right mixture of characteristics and traits. The proverbs teach us first about how to lead our own lives and then the way we should lead others. The ability of good leaders making sound decisions is what separates great leaders from their peers while gaining the respect of their followers.

Integrity

Integrity is a total commitment to the highest personal characteristics and professionalism with ethical standards. Leaders must first be honest and truthful in everything they do or the people they contact. Integrity means to establish a set of personal values and not compromising the position or the people under their command. Former Air Force Chief of Staff General Charles Gabriel said, "Integrity is the fundamental premise of military service in a free society. Without integrity, the moral pillars of our military strength, public trust, and self-respect lost." Proverbs teach the fundamental guiding principles of leadership, emphasizing the importance of integrity and value.

Great leaders seem to be above reproach and an unwilling will to be compromised and the ability to stay true to their values. What separates leaders, good leaders know the importance of integrity, and without it, they stand to lose the respect of their followers and superiors. The scriptures teach that every one of us can be a good leader, by having a solid foundation built on integrity, strong will to succeed, the right attitude, and drive to improve great leadership skills continuously can be achieved. The Book of Proverbs is a road map for leaders to use in improving their wisdom and built strong moral values based on integrity and staying faithful to God's Word.

Character is at the core of an al leader; leaders need to have high standards of moral character with traits of integrity, selflessness, and to strive for excellence in what they do. Leaders are entrusted with teaching and influencing their people, and teaching is not just a job but a critical profession that has lasting effects on pupils. Responsibility not only falls on leaders but parents and community leaders; they all must be active partners in by being positive role models and demonstrating firm leadership traits. One of the critical reasons the Roman Empire fell is because of integrity and morality in all aspects of society were compromised. Professionalism is characterized by the integrity to serve society and placing service before self. The rewards of and al leader come from knowing that they made a positive difference in the people around them.

Proverbs 22:6 provides valuable lessons for parents on how to be kind and just leaders for their people. Leaders and especially the parents play a crucial role in the development of the child, and it all starts with building character and by providing proper discipline. A child that has not been taught the fundamental basics of good character and disciplined at an early part of their lives will more than likely have deficiencies in these areas into adulthood. Discipline is the core building block of creating individuals with high integrity and moral values. Without discipline, everything is lost, especially in people; they need a structured upbringing that includes encouragement and positive role models.

Decisiveness

A willingness to act is what good leaders must do; they must have the self-confidence to make timely decisions. The leader must then effectively communicate the decision to their people. British Admiral Sir Roger Keyes emphasized that "In all operations, a moment arrives when brave decisions have an enterprise is to be carried through." Of course, decisiveness includes the willingness to accept responsibility. Leaders are always accountable--when things go right and when things go wrong.

The law of navigation teaches us to check the source of wisdom and motives while checking the outcomes. The leader provides the overall strategic planning for the school while promoting cooperation and teamwork with a vision towards mission accomplishment. The school leaders are responsible for creating the framework by which staff, faculty, and people interact with each other in implementing the goals within their environment. Leaders must promote a positive and nurturing culture that recognizes excellence in teaching and curriculum.

Selflessness

Good leaders sacrifice personal needs for the more significant cause of the many while ensuring mission accomplishment. General Douglas MacArthur said, "No action can safely trust its martial honour to leaders who do not maintain the universal code which distinguishes those things that are right and those things that are wrong." It requires courage and strength of character to deal with difficult situations, and great leaders confront tough situations head-on rather than avoiding or passing them on to others.

King Solomon issues a warning concerning a leader's authority and character, "When leaders try to exercise authority without a servant's heart, they eventually hurt themselves. Leaders add value by serving others" Ecclesiastes 8:1-9. Leaders need to be individuals of strong character and faith while putting God and people first above their ambitions and interests. Leaders should strive to keep safely in their hearts and soul their servitude to the higher authority of God. Leaders must not be conceited and vein because just as one rises to the top, they can as quickly fall; "The Lord giveth and the Lord taketh away" (Job 1:21). Leaders can lead without leading, and they can be silent and positive role models while at the same time realizing their limitations and recognizing the higher order of God's master plan.

Blackaby (2006) provided a story of selflessness when the evangelist known as Uncle Vasser exclaimed: "How glad I am to see the man that God has used to win so many souls to Christ!" In response, Moody stooped down and scooped up a handful of dirt. As he let the dust pour through his fingers, he confessed: "There is nothing more than that to D.L. Moody, except as God uses him!" Moody accepts his role as a servant before Him with God as his ultimate fountain of wisdom. No matter how much talent or skills one possesses, it does not compare to the power of the Lord, for He is responsible for all. Most insecure leaders mask their incompetence by brash and overpowering behaviour, but at their core, they are lost sheep in front of God. Wise leaders realize this and do not accept responsibilities for their success and always give praise to their people and God. Recently while watching a combat sporting event, one thing that most stood out much surprise after the fight the competitors thank God for all their accomplishments first. Despite the fame, God may give. It is essential to thank Him while looking towards Him for wisdom and His grand plan for existence.

According to Maxwell, "Leaders need to respond to individuals based on their needs rather than their faults. Proverbs 25-21-22 encourages us to see what others need, even our enemies, and respond accordingly." Individuals in any position of authority need to have a breadth of and experience in dealing with people. God has given all an individual conscience and different personalities, good leaders, realize this and adapt their leadership style based on the situation. Leaders, for example, may want to incorporate a more direct teaching approach with your people. In the higher levels of, a professor may be wise to use a lazier fair or participative style of leadership in order to accommodate the more advanced people.

Notes:

Leadership Principles

P roverbs teach al leaders valuable principles concerning ethical behaviour along with guidelines to develop practical leadership skills, character, and values based on a strong faith in God. Proverbs provide leaders with a moral foundation to lead with wisdom and intellect of a higher level. As leaders climb up the ladder of power, so does their abilities to make decisions narrow, with limited options except to choose the path of righteousness or risk it all and fail. Being a good leader means being fair and balanced in decision making and treating people with the utmost respect and dignity. Successful leaders see things before followers do; they see beyond what followers do, and they see bigger than followers do. While followers may barely feel able to see and plan beyond next week, leaders must think, envision, and plan well into the future.

Motivation

A most significant challenge is motivating subordinates to achieve the high standards set for them. Motivation is the key to successful leadership. Motivation is the moving force behind successful leadership. The ability to generate enthusiasm about the mission may be the most critical factor in leadership. Recognition of the efforts people put forth is one decisive way in which motivation toward mission accomplishment pays dividends. The leader who publicly applauds the efforts of unit personnel builds a cohesive organization, which will accomplish the mission.

Each person has a different personality style with varied learning and development abilities. These individual differences come in the form of intelligence and creativity; each one of us has a different capacity to process information and how we relate to one another. Motivation and attitude determine success; it is an internal state of mind that guides us towards higher achievement and goals. Solomon says, "he observes a person in a variety of context, and nothing seems to satisfy them" (Ecclesiastes 4:1-8). Successful leaders find ways to motivate people by capturing their level of interest and by building their confidence along with allowing then the freedom to express themselves.

Intrinsic motivation comes from internal factors that are within and can be controlled by the effort and devotion to the goal or task placed by the individual. On the other hand, extrinsic motivations are external factors that come in the form of reward and punishment that are outside the individual control. These motivation techniques are just part of the tools required for ineffective leadership and management of any situation or position of command. Individuals in a position of authority need to have a breadth of and experience in the areas of leadership, management, and psychology, especially personality typing. We all have different personalities, and the most effective leaders realize this and change their style of leading to fit the situation. For example, when. have new trainees with a little experience, a more direct approach while highly trained professions require a democratic style would be a better fit.

According to King Solomon, while observing people, he noticed the following concerning what motivates them, "They need comfort and fulfilment, completion and triumph, and consumption and greed." There is a lot more to leadership than meets the eye; it takes many years of experience to develop the whole person concept of being an active and understanding leader in understanding what makes people tick. One of the most effective management tools a leader can use is personality typing; these theories not only make a leader understand people better, but it also makes a leader learn more about themselves, and that is the key to effective leadership is to know oneself.

 Leaders help foster growth by insisting that their people stay focused and attentive to school lectures and projects. For people to be motivated and excel in school, leaders should create a challenging and positive environment for success. People must be allowed freedom and independence to be themselves for them to stay motivated and have a sense of the positive experience they can reflect in adult life. The role of the leaders in fostering student's growth and potential is to identify their weaknesses and strengths while looking for improvement opportunities and approaches. Ensure people progress permanently and positively while giving them goals and inspiration to try and do their best. Leaders' role is about encouraging people to set high standards for themselves. People need to know what is expected, and they need to be given the latitude to make a few mistakes for them to learn and mature.

Followership

The primary difference between leaders and followers is perspective. The primary difference between leaders is perspective, while both leaders and followers can have a strong character and can possess warm relational skills. Leaders and followers can even have a strong personality and a strong will, and what separates them is how they think and perceive reality. Because the scriptures teach, we are all made to rule, and everyone possesses the capacity to raise their level of leadership abilities. Everyone can improve their leadership skills and the approach they use in influencing others. We must, however, begin with a leadership perspective and that is the main ingredient that makes the Book of Proverbs so profound. Proverbs are about gaining wisdom and continually improving the thinking process and doing things smartly.

Professionalism

The word "professional" should inspire prospective and current leaders serving the community and people, with this status comes responsibility. Leaders play an essential part in the development and growth of people with lasting effects into adulthood. Furthermore, professionalism through continuous research, study, and experience in leading; leaders' role seems to fit firmly into this professional category. Professionalism is characterized by serving society and putting service before self; the rewards of teaching come from the knowledge of knowing that you made a positive difference in someone's life. Every leader has an obligation to their people to be the very best they can be. Leaders need to have high standards and moral values with leadership traits of integrity, selflessness, and to strive for excellence in what they do continuously. Leaders are entrusted with teaching and influencing our people, and it is not just a job but a critical profession that has lasting effects. Considering the demands placed upon leaders, society and community leaders need to recognize and reward them for their service and professionalism. The responsibility falls on not only the leaders but also the parents, and they must be active partners in

Communication

Former Air Force Chief of Staff General Thomas D. White believed, "Information is the essential link between wise leadership and purposeful action." Successful leaders listen to what their people have to say and are always looking for good ideas. It is the leader's job to keep all channels of communications open. The more senior a leader becomes the more listening skills they need. According to Proverbs 10:6-32, "The law of influence must have a skillful tongue. Several verses in Proverbs speak of the tongue and how to use it as a positive influence. Leaders who use words skillfully increase their influence." leaders need to be aware when they need to be silent and when to speak to truth in order to keep tranquility and peace around there influence of their research and work.

Leaders must take extra care when writing about religion and cultural differences that exist in the world, and it is their responsibility to mindful of the reaction if they write about controversial research topics. The law of influence demonstrates the need for a successful leader to have a skillful tongue. Leaders who use words skillfully increase their influence and understand the importance and power of their words. Which of the following best describes fair use of one's lips? Lips of the righteous bring forth wisdom, and they know what is acceptable while understanding the lips of the wicket as perverse.

According to Maxwell, "God rightly expects leaders to manage conflict within their organization." Proverbs 15: 1-7 provides valuable lessons for leaders to master their communication skills, and in turn, they will be better prepared to handle conflicts in their daily work. Communication is the lifeline of an organization; it determines how well people interact and work with each other. When lines of communications are severed, organizations struggle and eventually fail to meet their goals or accomplish their mission. The key to successful communications is to realize the importance of identifying various forms of communications and their application to fit the situation or place while applying them skillfully and wisely.

General of the Army Douglas MacArthur observed, "In no other profession are the penalties for employing untrained personnel so appalling or as irrevocable as in the military." Individuals in any position of authority need to have a breadth of and experience in the areas of leadership and management coupled with psychology training, especially personality typing. We all have different personalities, and the most effective leaders realize this and change their style of leading based on the situation.

For example, when having new trainees with no experience may want to use a more direct approach, while a mixture of individuals requires a democratic style. When faced with highly experienced individuals, a lazier fair-style would be a better fit. The problem with many institutions is they are quick to blame the individual and do not look at their system and processes; most people want to do a good job but when the system is dysfunctional; individuals efforts will only go so far and will eventually have a hard time succeeding and maybe set-up to fail.

Plato believed they should be used to plant the seed, the thirst of knowledge in order to have wise and capable rulers and leaders. Leaders should have many years of experience in the physical and mental realms for them to be just and ethical leaders. Plato describes the world in two dimensions of the visible and internal realms which consist of individual senses of the world around us and our inner soul or conscience. Plato continues the argument that justice on rational and educated thought processes represented by good rulers and individuals within a society. He also describes the opposite by irrational dictators that rule not by logic but for personal gains and interests while placing the needs of the people aside. The bottom line is that justice and goodness produce food for the souls of individuals, and the rulers for doing the opposite produce illness within the individual and produces hatred and destruction within societies.

Teamwork

Maslow's hierarchy of social needs involves emotionally based relationships, friendship, intimacy, and a supportive family. People need to feel they belong and within their group. Leaders provide the groundwork for making people feel accepted and part of the team. The feeling of acceptance provides confidence-building well into the future.

Providing people with opportunities for risk-taking teaches them valuable lessons in that they will, in many situations, not be able to succeed, but with extra effort and a positive attitude, they will eventually succeed. Leaders should provide an environment where the people learn by their mistakes and that it is acceptable to repeat a topic many times over until completed. Repetition is an excellent way for people to hone their skills without fearing of failure and punishment. Lessons learned by risk-taking help teens build confidence into adulthood and make them realize that not everything mastered without hard work.

Maslow's hierarchy of social needs is a theory in psychology proposed by Abraham Maslow in his paper "A Theory of Human Motivation" that involves emotionally based relationships, for example, friendship, intimacy, and supportive family. People need to feel they belong within their group. Team members need to find ways to work well together and to make each other feel accepted and part of the team. The feeling of acceptance provides confidence building will help them be more successful in accomplishing their goal or task and help in developing well into the future.

Maslow's hierarchy of needs is achieved by progressive and logical order of importance, consisting of a pyramid with five levels. The pyramid starts with the lowest level of physiological needs, while the top-level is associated with self-actualization needs. The higher needs in this hierarchical pyramid only achieved when the lower needs are met when the individual moves to the next higher level the lower level will no longer be a priority.

Leader provides the overall strategic planning for the school while promoting cooperation and teamwork. The organizational leaders are responsible for creating the framework for people and how they interact with each other in implementing the goals within their work environment. Leaders must promote a positive and nurturing culture that recognizes excellence. Many professions rely on teamwork as an example in the military environment. If the team fails, the mission fails also. Individuals in the military contribute to the overall mission by sharing their knowledge and expertise.

There are many situations where an individual may have more knowledge about a topic, and they are not willing to share or help their fellow teammates because they feel a sense of power from the knowledge they possess. Teamwork and sharing of information with one another not only provide you with a positive feeling of knowing that. Helped someone, but it also creates a positive environment of sharing and trust that can be used to accomplish the task or mission more effectively and efficiently. We need to look at smarter ways to help people work better together and not place heavy emphasis on inspections and assessments.

Risk-taking helps a student learn more efficiently, and it plays a significant role in moving them through the next stage of development. Additionally, leaders need to be risk-takers also while applying different approaches to teaching with continuous improvements gained by experience in dealing with all types of people and situations. Applying different teaching techniques in the classroom stimulates and engages the people's willingness to learn. Also, integration of technology in the classroom is crucial in student development; with rapid advances in science and technology, people need to stay abreast in order to prepare for the workplace.

Providing people with opportunities to practice teaches them valuable lessons that they would be able to use in similar situations as they arise. Teams need an environment where they can simulate real-life situations and be able to learn by their mistakes and to be able to repeat a topic many times over until they feel comfortable and get it done right.

Repetition is an excellent way for people to hone their skills without fearing of failure and punishment. Lessons learned by experimental work while working in teams help people build confidence and make them realize that everything learned with effort and the right attitude.

People learn best by doing and solving problems while at the same time, it is essential for them to play an active role in their learning. It is also helpful for people to work in small groups and share ideas and information through open discussion. Brainstorming sessions are one of the tools that can be used to help people get involved and it motivates them to contribute their ideas and theories in order to find the best possible solutions. Each student in a group motivated in different ways but most of the time, the enthusiasm and organization of the team determine the success and participation of each member of the team. Team members develop a rapport with each other, and the team leader has the responsibility to provide guidance and vision towards the goal while creating an environment of trust, sense of belonging, and purpose.

Know Oneself

Knowing one self-own strength and weaknesses is critical to effective leadership. The leader must be able to recognize their capabilities and limitations. Former Chief Master Sergeant of the Air Force Robert D. Gaylor put it this way: "Sure, everyone wants to be an effective leader, whether it is in the Air Force or the community. Can one identify strengths, capitalize on them, and consciously strive to reduce and minimize the times apply style inappropriately?"

In Proverbs 8, The Law of Intuition teaches that wisdom makes a difference between mediocre and great leaders. Great leaders see things overall and big-picture view while always thinking and planning the next move like chess masters in the game of life. Leadership requires understanding and the willingness to have the right state of mind and a positive attitude in line with the teachings of the scriptures. The scriptures provide the road map towards success, and history has proven over and over those leaders that go astray always find themselves on the short end of the stick, while many pays with their lives. Great leaders rely on wisdom and always try not to repeat the failures of the past while staying on the path of righteousness.

It is easy to conclude that it is challenging for leaders to control or change people around them. Sure, they can use their position power to direct people under their command, but this is real leadership. Leaders need to be highly ethical individuals with higher standards of integrity and moral values. Leaders in a position of authority that has lasting effects for the people they lead. Leaders need to follow in God's footsteps and be humble in their leadership approach in dealing with the people under their command.

Notes:

Leadership Styles

An individual's personality is usually formed by the age of seven and even earlier. Individuals are influenced by parents and external factors that include peer pressure and their surrounding environment. Parents play a vital role in the success of their people from an early age, and many habits formed during this stage of development that can influence an individual's leadership habits well into adulthood. It is understood that to know oneself is to be a better leader. While attending the Air Force Senior Leadership School, what discovered was that in order to be an effective leader, one must make changes in their personality in order to fit the person or people lead. It is challenging to implement on the job because as a leader has given authority over people and making changes within self does not fit with the common perception of what a leader stands for. This report will analyze different leadership behavioral styles; several different tools used to measure characteristics and behaviour leadership and management styles.

I am not sure if can teach leadership, but good leaders realize change and continuous adjustments in personality and character is the key to success. General Patton once said, "one is on parade every day," meaning that superiors and subordinates watch every move made. Character is something gained from an early age and influenced by family, friends, and society, and it is part of the personality. Most of us are born with a sound mind, and we intrinsically know from right and wrong, when it comes down to making the right choices. Leadership and character go together and will know, especially when they are faced with difficult situations while making hard decisions. Choose the route of least resistance, or will the right decision based on a strong character based on traits of integrity, honesty, and courage.

Team dynamics include complex interactions between team members while influencing their behaviour and performance. Many forces affect teams; to include different personality styles and types, friendships, relationships, equipment, facilities and design, external influences, senior leaders and managers and many more. All these factors influence a team in many positive and negative ways. The success of the team will be determined by how well the team will be able to manage and overcome many issues that are part of team dynamics. According to the Target Training International leadership and management survey responses, the report has selected general statements to provide a broad understanding of his work style. These statements identify the basic natural behaviour that he brings to the job. That is, if left on his own, these statements identify HOW HE WOULD CHOOSE TO DO THE JOB. Use the general characteristics to gain a better understanding of natural behaviour."

Many different types of personality and charter styles of leadership and management tools have been successfully used in government and the business world to build a team. Team dynamics are influenced by many factors to include conditions, organization, team goals, and a different mix of personalities of the group. Each team member brings his own experiences and cultural background to the team, potentially causing misunderstanding of thought while at the same time, it could be a real source of energy with various ideas.

Teams eventually build an identity of their own, stemming from the interrelationship of individuals from different backgrounds and cultures with each team member bringing individual experience and qualities of their own. Within the team, individual team members have specific roles and work to perform; each member brings specific influence on the team. When another individual replaces team composition changes, and for example, one team member leaves and then, the team dynamics have to re-shuffle to create a new identity. When team members understand each other, it makes it easier for them to share experiences and expertise, resulting in better performance for the entire team.

Personality differences have shown to provide better results because each member brings his different thoughts and ideas to the table thus helping make smarter decisions and choices. The team needs to make sure it spends time at the start of the project or task to go over details of the plan and how they are going to approach the work while formulating a strategy in order to accomplish the mission goals. Successful teams eventually build a state of synergy that helps then achieve high levels of accomplishment and success.

Stephen Covey's book called 7 Habits of Highly Effective People defines Synergy as "The whole is greater than the sum of the parts." All successful individuals and teams realize the importance of synergy. Teams that do not develop synergy have a difficult time accomplishing their goals and tasks, while struggling to coexist with each other. The question is, are team members working well together and supporting each other? If they are not, their chances of success are diminished, and on the other hand, if they are jelling and clicking like seconds on a clock, then their chances of success are very likely. Synergy is like a tornado once it starts; it continues to grow to bring success upon success to the team and its members.

According to Target Training International "Research has proven that job-related talents are directly related to job satisfaction and personal performance. People are well-positioned to achieve success when they are engaged in work suited to their inherent skills, behavioral style, and unique values. And, all teams need to be made up of the right mix of people, each contributing in their own way. In addition, insights on how to communicate effectively to customers, employees, and business partners with different styles are very important. The foundation for designing the organization or business around strengths and passion, so that become a more effective leader and produce the results with the organization. This report analyzes the behavioral style; that is, a person's manner of doing things."

A trait is a stable characteristic and is something lasting throughout one's entire life. The difficulty is coming up with an exact list that characterizes leadership traits. Culture plays a major role; people from different walks of life have a different set of values and beliefs that influence their decision making. Character defies logic, and it is due to the subconscious factors, and on emotions. A person's character and leadership qualities focus on behaviour and goals and outcomes. It is reasonable to assume that character and personality traits are associated with leadership, while others are not. Many times, we focus on character and leadership traits associated with success, but it is interesting to understand failures of leadership as well. Some leaders forget about the goal and concentrate on themselves instead of the whole. Good leaders understand the importance of good communications; people need to know the plan, and they need to know. Many leaders are afraid of bucking the system and go along with the program, even though it may be at the expense of subordinates. It is also essential that the leaders are in good physical, psychological, emotional and spiritual shape.

Most employees in management and leadership positions have received quality leadership and management training of some sort. On my own experience in the Air Force, during the early 1990s, the Air Force leadership pushed for quality management and leadership training across all levels within the military command. We received intensive training and for several years and attempted to restructure the way we did business; with the idea of continuous improvement and to accomplish this, we used various quality tools like statistics, benchmarks, self-evaluations, and surveys to name a few.

The biggest obstacle to implementing the quality initiatives was an individual's resistance to change; people had been doing something the same way for many years, and suddenly, they are asked to change. To say the least, it was a painful process for most, and from my own experience I would submit recommendations saving in the millions, instead of embracing my proposals that where based on real facts and statistics, I was beaten up along the way and people resented the idea of someone making these recommendations for change. When it comes to it, change is difficult and requires constant hard work and a different way of thinking – the continuous improvement process is not an easy road and takes many years to achieve, and it is not an overnight process. Governments and individuals in high command positions have the tools available to them, and it is their choice to use them to make things better.

Summary of Personal Traits Regarding decision-making strategies According to Target Training International leadership and management survey results, "I prefer an environment with variety and change. He is at his best when many projects are underway at once. He likes people but can occasionally see as cold and blunt. He may have his mind on project results and sometimes may not take the time to be empathetic toward others. He prefers being a team player and wants each player to contribute along with him. His sensitivity to errors and mistakes sometimes tempers his aggressiveness. He accused of being "work compulsively" because of these tendencies. Deadline conscious and becomes irritated if deadlines are delayed or missed. He likes to be forceful and direct when dealing with others. His desire for results is readily apparent to the people he manages. He can be blunt and critical of people who do not meet his standards. To come up with new ideas and follow them through to completion. It may not trust others to do his projects, especially if they have displayed an inability to perform to his standards. At times, he may be reluctant to delegate specific tasks. He is a creative person and uses this creativity to solve problems."

Notes:

Military Leadership Perspective

The Air Force enlisted promotion testing consists of two separate programs: Promotion Fitness Examination and Specialty Knowledge Tests. Individuals working within their specialty are eligible to compete for promotions. Selection for promotion includes not only the highest scores of both the PFE and SKT exams but also the time in service, time in rank, performance reports, and decorations are all included in the final tally to determine individuals with the highest scores and recommendation for promotion based on limited pre-determined quotas.

The evaluation board considers all aspects of an individual demonstrating the qualities of being a good leader. A key factor under review is the capability of an individual to move to a higher supervisory and management role based on the Air Force concept of a whole-person. When recruits enter military service, they are placed under an extreme environment wholly closed off from their civilian life, setting the stage for new habits. The authoritarian approach is needed while dealing with recruits in order to establish acceptable behavioral norms and attitudes following fulfilling military mission requirements. Recruits are subjugating to a daily routine that is closely monitored every step of the way to ensure compliance and training progression through various activities and exams. This harsh authoritarian setting either makes or breaks an individual; while many do adopt and graduate, there is the exception that some either give up or are not cut out for this type of training. Most experts would agree that it is essential for new military recruits to experience a highly disciplined do-or-die situation, considering the nature of the military profession, although recruits are strictly learning followership skills, introduced to higher forms of leadership building either through observation or playing roles of team leaders within their ranks.

So, recruits are pressured continuously to take orders either from their instructors or through indirect peer pressure and various team-building activities. The individual is left with minimal choices and must follow or fall out of favour from their instructors and fellow team members. Using direct external motivational strategies, which include instructor and peer pressure, it is easier and quicker to train recruits for more advanced instruction. As military members progress towards higher rank and authority, approached with a participative style of leadership, except direct orders or combat situations requiring quick on the spot actions. The military promotion ladder is a very well outlined and structured process that integrates experience and professional training and throughout one's career. Everyone is aware and knows what they must do in order to move up in rank, and this establishes the ground rules allowing for individuals to be extrinsically and intrinsically self-motivated to work and study harder in order to climb higher the promotion ladder

What are the implications of leadership and management in a school setting? Leaders are leaders by steering the people towards a common goal in pursuit of practical. While classroom management is more concerned with resources, efficiency, and planning. To be successful, leaders need both leadership and management and find ways of balancing the two. For a leader with strong leadership and with weak management skills is no better, and sometimes worse, than the opposite. The challenge is to achieve a balance of strong leadership and secure management. Proper management brings a degree of order and consistency for people; they know their place in the classroom, the chair they sit on, and their need to feel safe and secure. However, people need leaders with strong leadership skills to guide them and have a positive influence on them while helping them build stable character traits.

The comparison of successful leaders and managers comes down to that neither type of behaviour is better than the other. Leaders must have a grasp of management and leadership skills to be successful. Moreover, leadership and management go hand in hand, and the two should work in harmony. In other words, leadership is an art form that also includes management skills to be most effective. The best managers tend to become ethical leaders more because they develop leadership abilities with time and the skills required using proper management techniques. Also, it is seldom that an effective leader is not a good manager; both bring a sense of balance. Successful leaders bring a human touch to management with skills of motivating, influencing, and provide inspirational motivation.

The following words are from military leaders of the past that many of us can learn from and be able to integrate into our own lives and influence people. There is no difference between military leadership and the leadership required to manage and lead a classroom. There is no magic formula when it comes to successful leadership; every leader has his style of leading. He has some outgoing leaders and others who are reserved, and they are both successful leaders in their way. It seems that the best thing to do when it comes to leadership and management is to be yourself and enjoy the moment with your people.

A leader is responsible for creating a positive and nurturing culture that promotes growth and professionalism. The leader places the safety and security of the people and the staff above all while managing the day to day activities of the organization. A leader plays a pivotal role in mobilizing resources towards establishing special programs and diverse cultural initiatives. The culture of an organization seems to influence the behaviour of individuals or groups within their environment or society.

Many experts agree that successful organizations have one common trait; they are made up of a culture that respects diversity and places high expectations on their people. Leaders must be aware of the climate of their culture affects the morale and productivity of not only the people but the staff and leaders. If leaders desire to improve the curriculum and systems, they must create a positive and supportive environment that strives to enhance the school's culture.

Leaders need to recognize the organizational culture of an organization by emphasizing values, character, integrity, and practical goal setting in order to define further what they stand for. Many describe culture as the glue that holds the organization together, expressing the social values and beliefs individuals share. In organization environments, culture sets the tone for people and leaders alike; creating a culture that encourages a trusting and sharing environment is the goal all leaders should strive. Every organization has its feel and culture-specific to the people involved within their environment. It is essential to have effective leaders that portray confidence and leadership abilities with solid values and ideals. Values and ideals from above are sometimes tricky to instill, but the norms of the organization will reflect the actual values and ideals of the people. The idea is for management to have buy-in by the people in the mission and the goals of the organization. Leaders can place expectations and sanctions on individuals in order to align their interests following the values and ideals of the organization.

Active institutions have a clear set of cultural elements that emphasize values of academic effort and achievement. This is accomplished by applying high expectations that stress individual excellence and performing exceeding potentials. Leaders can use encouragement and rewards for high performing individuals while discouraging disorderly conduct. Effective leaders have high expectations and the attitude that any student is capable of achievement regardless of social class or past performance. Successful organization culture promotes self-improvement by leaders through continues and training and experimentation with far more effective work methods and processes. In addition, it is important for the organization culture to encourage worker participation in various activities thus promoting the total person concept. It is important to know that organizational cultures are not static and are always evolving into many forms and shapes depending on the environment and the people involved.

Hierarchical Organization Structure

The organizational leadership traits of the Air National Guard squadrons' commander and his staff correctly demonstrated role schemas by effectively applying the correct decisions to fit the situation. The squadron commander and his personnel are legally bound and required to follow military directives and orders from higher headquarters concisely and accurately. The units' leaders are consistent in their decision making while demonstrating characteristics trait schemas of emotional stability, enthusiasm, conscientiousness, tough-mindedness, and self-assurance.

Developing the right characteristics in the employees was a priority for the squadron commander and his staff. Also, creating a conceptual complete military member based on a whole person concept, while integrating traits of integrity, selflessness, and loyalty as part of an ideal military member and leader. While many experts may not agree on what constitutes excellent characteristics in an individual, can assume that you are doing something right if you have followers who exhibit respect, confidence, and loyal cooperation. The following traits are considered essential to building character and are directly linked to effective leadership; selflessness, decisiveness, energy, commitment, loyalty, and integrity. Leadership traits linked to personality traits and successful leaders tend to have the following personality characteristics; emotional stability, enthusiasm, conscientiousness, tough-mindedness, and self-assurance.

During a discussion with the Commander of the Air National Guard Squadron concerning how his unit dealt with individuals with perceptual distortions and what measures are in place to ensure individuals and teams focused on the right direction towards meeting mission objectives. The Commander went on and discussed the matter concerning one of his senior noncommissioned officers working in the workload control center.

Due to the many observations and reporting, as an Air Force advisor, on the irrational and unprofessional behaviour of the workload controller, that he was left with a minimal choice and had to act and deal with the situation in a direct manner. The position with the Commander and the Air National Guard unit was only in an advisory role concerning technical matters and the overall organizational health of the unit and not on matters of disciplinary actions.

The Commander proceeded to counsel the workload controller on several occasions concerning her irrational behaviour and poor decision-making skills. He also told the workload controller that her actions are affecting the overall moral or the troops along with a breakdown in communications between different groups and sections of the Squadron.

The Commander correctly pointed out that the workload controllers mostly relied on her emotions on making decisions required in a very structured and logical manner following military customs and standards. In other words, if, for instance, the workload controller did not like at a personnel level, she would place you in the least desired projects or would double up higher ranking individuals to share the same accommodations. The workload controller had a completely distorted perception of her position by a sense of being control-oriented beyond normalcy.

After many months of anguishing to decide and noticing little change in irrational behaviour and distorted attitude of the workload controller, the commander decided to take on a different approach and invited the base chaplain to assist with the matter. After several weeks the commander invited and other senior members of the organization to listen to the findings of the chaplain. In short, the chaplain agreed the workload controller had personality issues and finally said, "may God help you." as he walked away. Several weeks later, the higher command was heavily involved, and the workload controller reassigned to a different organization working with fewer people in the role of managing supplies.

Studies demonstrate the distorted perception of individuals or groups affects the organization and it is up to senior management to take immediate action before matters escalate to severe conflict. Perception determines behaviour and how people see things and in turn, how they behave and act within their circle of friends and work environment. If an individual's reality distorted, so will their personnel life, along with their job, will also be distorted. Distorted perception and poor judgment of a single individual can affect the entire group and, in many instances, the entire organization, depending on the role or position held by the individual within the chain of command or hierarchy of the unit. Individuals with distorted perception at lower levels do effect have some effect on other team members within the group and have less of an impact on the rest of the organization.

The biggest challenge is in situations of individuals with distorted perceptions in higher positions within the chain of command of an organization. It becomes more challenging to have these individuals seek counselling or fired from their positions. Organizations need to have in place policies and procedures in dealing with individuals with distorted perceptions, no matter how high the position within the organizational chain of command. Although the unit had the issue of the workload controller and her distorted reality, removal from her position was a behavioral problem and not about biases or discriminatory.

From the point of view, after observing the Air National Guard unit for over three years, the overall racial environment and organizational stability were highly professional and fair in every aspect. Concerning individual and or group biases or prejudice within and between different sections of the organization were nonexistent, while everyone appeared relaxed and pleased working in the squadron. Military regulations and policies concerning equal opportunity are apparent and precise; every member has treated equally no matter gender, race, and personnel beliefs if it did not interfere with mission accomplishment.

The military structure does not tolerate discrimination, and this policy was very apparent at maintaining a high state of readiness for the Air National Guard unit. As in any organization, it is impossible to control an individual's personnel beliefs and how they have been brought up. Because of the shared mass of the military branches of service, there have been documented cases of sexual harassment and racial misconduct. Based on observations, none of these issues affected the Air National Guard unit for the duration of the tour; everyone within the organization treated each other in a respectful and highly professional matter. Another consideration to consider is that the Air National Guard unit located in a multicultural city in northern California. The Air National Guard unit also directly reflected the cities multicultural composition which comprised the unit with many different races along with the female-male ratio of workers represented. The squadrons' cross-cultural attitude is extremely positive and highly progressive for the organization, most of the individuals that contacted welcomed the multi-cultural make-up of the unit. Besides, squadron records did not have any instances of racial or cross-cultural issues, except for a few instances of personality conflicts.

The power for developing and encouraging learning within an organization relies on effective strategies for encouraging creativity and a higher order of thinking. The Air National Guard unit uses various in-house and formal training methods for educating its members. According to the Air National Guard training manager, he is responsible for maintaining a database of all unit members that include task and supervisory qualifications. The training manager also schedules and coordinates all training and requirements for the members of the organization. In-house training conducted on a needed basis on many different skills sets and or management and leadership type enhancement seminars. Then Air National Guard units and its members are required to maintain high levels of skills in order to maintain their mission readiness status for their states and the Air Force.

The structured training and program of the military, on a tiered skill level progression, inherently encourage individuals to be self-motivated for higher achievement in developing their skills and honing their leadership and management capabilities. The formal training for Air National Guard members starts with basic military training on listed troops and then consists of the technical training school, and after successful completion of these two programs, individuals sent back to their units. Upon arrival to their duty assignment, individuals are placed on a self-study program to enhance their duty position and skills further.

The technical aspect of this training continues until members achieve professional skill levels. In addition to the technical training individual members also must complete a series of supervisory and management courses in residence and correspondence. Military members, in general, are regularly required to train and educate, not only in military matters but also are encouraged to attend and pursue further tool colleges and universities of their choice. Leaders can make a tremendous difference in sharing their al experience while encouraging you and less-seasoned military members to further their technical skills and pursue higher.

Although informal and formal training al methods are essential for teaching theory, the real learning comes from actual on-the-job, hands-on field experience. What separates a great leader and supervisor from an ineffective one, and ethical leadership encourages cooperation and collaboration between members of a team. Effective leaders are continuously working towards ensuring their followers trained, and they accomplished this by sharing their knowledge and experience while adequately demonstrating special techniques and skills to the individuals within their team. Leadership is about motivating people to accomplish the mission. While it is the leader's responsibility to train their people effectively, it is also the responsibility of the followers to be attentive and ready to learn in order to improve their skills and overall capabilities.

Based on several years of observation, the unit commander and his management staff use various modelling techniques for demonstrating the organization's overall missions and strategies. These information dissemination modelling techniques and methods include informal and formal procedures that consist of direct face-to-face conversations, phone calls, e-mails, bulletin boards, unit newsletters, and organizational strategic plans — most of the information concerning mission-critical projects within special face-to-face meetings in the organization's conference room. The workload controller's office is responsible for obtaining projects from higher headquarters and assigning teams for implementation.

Each section superintendent receives the projects from the workload controller and then assigns the appropriate teams based on skillset qualifications and personnel requirements. The team chiefs and their team members review the project and make appropriate corrections to the engineering section if required. Once the project review process completed, the team is ready to start a pre-implementation survey and then implement the project. During the entire project cycle, the superintendents, workload controller, and the commander and his staff continually updated and briefed on the status of the projects. The organizational modelling structure for informational and data dissemination and gathering process are highly efficient and reliable.

There are several modelling strategies devoted to increasing productivity and improving individual performance, which tend to shape the organizational structure and focus. These three major strategic orientations, which are useful in planning and managing organizational change, include empirical rational, power coercive and normative reductive strategies. The empirical rational strategy includes personal selections and replacements which require early-retirement, dismissal, transfers, and reorganization of organizational members. The Air National Guard units' personnel status, according to the commander, is always on constant alert to maintain their workforce levels. Due to retirements and separation of unit members, the Air National Guard squadron is in continues recruiting mode to attract and enlist new members. In times of war or crises, the unit commander has relied on his position power to maintain his members from separating from the Air National Guard. Overall the Air National Guard units as demonstrated a flexible culture that is resilient in successfully dealing with internal and external mission requirements.

Diversity in an organizational workforce can be a vital source for merging various talents in which different cultures and personalities come together in creating new ideas and thought processes. Observations of the Air National Guard unit divided into many different work centers with their identity and tasking. For example, particularly this Air National Guard Squadron is responsible for installing telecommunications systems in support of Air Force and DoD customers.

The organization is led by the squadron commander and his deputy officers who are responsible for the maintenance and operations sections. Under the leadership of the deputy officers, noncommissioned officers are considered superintendents of the fights and the team leaders. Unit flights consist of different work sections, which consist of the radio, antenna, cable, and various other sections. In addition to the various sections that make up a squadron, there are numerous different skills sets and qualifications that are required to have a fully operational organization. The biggest challenge facing this squadron and many other units throughout the Air National Guard and Air Forces maintain a fully qualified and trained workforce. Most troops depart from military service after their first term; this vacuum creates a constant and continuous requirement for recruits along with all the training required to have a fully qualified workforce.

When the squadron commander asked about the most challenging part of being a leader, he believed the most significant challenge for a leader was the ability to motivate people, motivating people may be the most challenging part of leadership. On the other hand, the training manager thought that the most challenging part of being a leader is in dealing with the diversity in personalities, each person has a different personality style with varied learning and development abilities. Several lower-ranking troops, when questioned about what motivates them to be more productive, took a moment to gather their thoughts and agreed that the single most motivating factor was their concern for their fellow team members and their leader. They felt out of respect for the team that they had to perform at a high level and not let their fellow team members down.

These discussions proved that individual differences come in the form of intelligence and creativity; each one of us has a different capacity to process information and how we relate to one another. Motivation and attitude determine success; it is an internal state of mind that guides us towards higher achievement and goals. Intrinsic motivation comes from internal factors that are within and can be controlled by the effort and devotion to the goal or task placed by the individual. On the other hand, extrinsic motivations are external factors that come in the form of reward and punishment that are outside the individual control. These motivation techniques are just part of the tools required for ineffective leadership and management of any situation or position of command. The thing that stands out most is the concern of everyone for the overall wellbeing of the other members of the team. Successful leaders realize that they cannot accomplish the mission alone and need the support of their people in order to be successful. Good leaders sacrifice personal needs for the more significant cause of the many while ensuring mission accomplishment.

Just as any individual working for an organization would have a personal set of goals and specific challenges, so to do members of the Air National Guard Squadron have their own individual goals and specific challenges. It would be difficult to learn or measure individual goals, except for specific work-related challenges and goals. For instance, the Air Force enlisted promotion testing system motivates individuals to set goals and specific challenges the words moving up the ranks. The Air Force enlisted promotion testing consists of two separate programs: Promotion Fitness Examination (PFE) and Specialty Knowledge Tests (SKT). Individuals working within their specialty are eligible to compete for promotions. Having they will structure a promotion system allows military members to better plan and focus on setting personal goals and specific challenges towards achieving their objectives. The military promotion ladder is a very well outlined and structured process that integrates experience and professional training and throughout one's career. Everyone is aware and knows what they must do in order to move up in rank, and this establishes the ground rules allowing for individuals to be extrinsically and intrinsically self-motivated to work and study harder in order to climb higher the promotion ladder.

The Air National Guard squadron has a good structure awards and decorations program for acknowledging outstanding individual performance. The awards and decorations program follow established Air Force regulations in which the commander and his staff must follow in detail. In most situations, the squadron's awards and decorations program is consistent, recognizing individuals who go above and beyond the call of duty. A significant problem with the entire military awards and decorations program is that it relies on individual in supervisory and management positions to write them, which require a high standard and useful writing abilities to include many hours to accomplish. Some leaders do take the time and effort to accomplish the awards and decorations reports, while many do not take the extra time to write them. So, the Air Force awards, and decorations program counts on leaders to adequately reward their people. The awards and decorations, in most instances, are not equitable and lack consistency, and for this, most of the troops throughout the ranks do not consider them as part of their reasons for motivating them to do a better job. On the other hand, most do appreciate rewarded for their efforts, and others do not need a pat on the back because they have the confidence in themselves to do a good job.

Personality differences determine if extra benefits and incentives motivate an individual. Some individuals need constant reminders that they are doing a great job, while others could care less about external motivational incentives and are self-motivated in accomplishing their day-to-day activities. Wise leaders recognize individual differences and alter and tailor-fit their leadership styles to fit the individuals under their command. From observing the senior noncommissioned officers of the Air National Guard squadron, it was apparent that their vast experience in dealing with people that they effectively-recognized outstanding performers and thus appropriately provided them with the recognition they deserved. Although the senior noncommissioned officers were efficient in rewarding good behaviour, they were also quick in disciplining and correcting individuals that were subpar and problematic.

A leadership trait is a stable characteristic and is something lasting throughout one's working career. The difficulty is coming up with an exact list that characterizes leadership traits since culture plays a significant role as people from different walks of life have a different set of values and beliefs that influence their decision making. A person's character and leadership qualities focus on behaviour and goals and outcomes. Culture also played an essential role in the Air National Guard's commander leadership style and the traits he had developed over the years; since his background was of Japanese heritage, his traits based on honour, integrity, selflessness, and loyalty. The commander highly respected amongst the troops for his dedicated efforts in ensuring everyone in the organization treated equally and fairly. The commanders' approach towards leadership set the stage for his staff and the entire organization to uphold a righteous path, where honesty and integrity received center stage.

Managers use the process to control people and material, leaders, on the other hand, try to motivate and inspire people in the right direction. In order to be successful, leaders help their subordinates feel a sense of belonging, recognition and build their self-esteem. The overall leadership of the Air National Guard squadron is effectively using their roles and position power to manage and lead the activities of their sections. After the arrival of the new workload controller, the organizational moral was highly positive, and the overall health of the organization was evident as the channels of communication between different sections vastly improved. The terminated workload controller inappropriately used her position power and many circumstances, abused her position power, which crippled the effectiveness of the organization. It demonstrates the importance of a leader's ability to make effective decisions and lead in a sound and appropriate manner while recognizing the importance of their position and power in the overall effect on the health and stability of their organization. Management involves power by position and leadership involves power by influence and the relationship between leadership and management to go hand in hand, while deploying effective management should possess leadership skills and effective leaders should demonstrate excellent management skills. Leading is an art that takes years to perfect and acquire, and it involves the power of being able to influence people for a common goal.

References

Boorse, D. (2003). OVERPOPULATION: ECOLOGICAL AND BIBLICAL PRINCIPLES

CONCERNING LIMITATION. Worldviews: Environment Culture Religion, 7(1/2), 154.

Retrieved from EBSCOhost.

Brown, M. (1982). Biblical Myth and Contemporary Experience: The Akedah in Modern Jewish

Literature. Judaism, 31(1), 99. Retrieved from EBSCOhost.

Csinos, D. M. (2010). "Come, Follow Me": Apprenticeship in Jesus' Approach to .

Religious, 105(1), 45-62. DOI:10.1080/00344080903472725

Chia, P. (2006). Local and Global: Biblical Studies in a "Runaway World". In, Sino- Religious

Studies (pp. 83-106). Chung Yuan Religious University. Retrieved from EBSCOhost.

Gericke, J. W. (2010). THE HEBREW SCRIPTURES IN CONTEMPORARY PHILOSOPHY OF

RELIGION. Verbum et Ecclesia, 31(1), 1-6. DOI:10.4102/ve.v31i1.395

John C. Maxwell, 2007, The Maxwell Leadership scriptures, Lessons in Leadership from the Word

of God, Second Edition

Fiorenza, E. (2003). Rethinking the al Practices of Biblical Doctoral Studies. Teaching

Theology & Religion, 6(2), 65-75. DOI:10.1111/1467-9647.00156

Lee, B. (2007). When the Text Is the Problem: A Postcolonial Approach to Biblical Pedagogy.

Religious, 102(1), 44-61. DOI:10.1080/00344080601117689

Toom, T. (2009). Hermeneutics: Principles and Processes of Biblical Interpretation – By Henry

A. Virkler and K. Gerber Ayayo. Reviews in Religion & Theology, 16(2), 318-321.

DOI:10.1111/j.1467-9418.2008.00425_4.x

Wickett, R. Y. (2002). Biblical Covenants, Learning Covenants, and Theological.

British Journal of Theological, 12(2), 154. Retrieved from EBSCOhost.

Air Force Instruction (AFI) 38-101 (2011), Manpower and Organization Air Force

The organization, Retrieved from www.e-publishing.af.mil

Air Force Pamphlet (AFP) 36-2241 (2011), Professional Development Guide,

Retrieved from: www.e-publishing.af.mil

Owens, R. G., & Valesky T. C. (2009). Organizational behavior in: Adaptive

leadership and school reform (9th ed.). Boston, MA: Pearson Inc.

The Maxwell Leadership scriptures, Lessons in Leadership from the Word of God by John C.

Maxwell, September 18, 2007

Hackman, Michael Z. and Johnson, Craig E. Leadership: A Communication Perspective Prospect

Heights, 5th Edition, IL: Waveland Press Inc., 2008. (ISBN-13: 9781577665793)

Kouzes, James M. and Posner, Barry Z. The Leadership Challenge San Francisco, 4th Edition,

CA: Jossey-Bass Inc., 2008 (ISBN-13: 9780787984922)

Schultz, Glen. Kingdom: God's Plan for Educating Future Generations Nashville, 2nd

Edition, TN: LifeWay Press, 2003. (ISBN 0-6330-9130-8)

Official Army Leadership Definitions, 1987, Retrieved from

http://www.au.af.mil/au/awc/awcgate/army/cmd-hdbk-appa.pdf

The Official Web site of the United States Air Force, 2011,

http://www.af.mil/information/bios/bio.asp?bioID=7618

Kouzes, James M. and Posner, Barry Z. The Leadership Challenge San Francisco, 4th Edition, CA: Jossey-Bass Inc., 2008 (ISBN-13: 9780787984922)

http://www.au.af.mil/au/awc/awcgate/army/cmd-hdbk-appa.pdf

http://www.af.mil/information/bios/bio.asp?bioID=7618

John C. Maxwell, 2007, The Maxwell Leadership scriptures, Lessons in Leadership from the Word of God, Second Edition.

Henry and Richard Blackaby (2006) Spiritual Leadership, The Interactive Study, Published by

Broadman and Holman Publishers, Nashville, Tennessee.

Ronald W. Rebore, 2001, The Ethics of al Leadership, Merril Prentice Hall

Wikipedia, the free encyclopedia, 2010, Twelve O'clock High, Retrieved March 26, 2010, from

https://en.wikipedia.org/wiki/Twelve_O'Clock_High

Hoy, W. K., & Miskel, C. G. (2008). al administration: Theory, research, and

practice (8th ed.). New York: McGraw-Hill

Amanda Reavy (2011), SPOTLIGHT: Ill. institutions aim to reduce bullying, Mar. 27, 2011,

Retrieved from http://www.bnd.com/2011/03/27/1646844/spotlight-ill-institutions-aim-to-reduce.html

Maxwell, J. C., & Elmore, T. (2007). The Maxwell leadership scriptures: Lessons in leadership from the word of God (2nd ed.). Nashville: Thomas Nelson.

Target Training International, Ltd. (1984-2008) the Alternative Board, Belmar, NJ

Website sources:

http://www.colemanennis.com/fre-leadership-style-report/Default.aspx?RewriteStatus=1

Robert M. Galford and Regina Fazio Maruca (2006), Leadership Styles Assessment Test. r

Leadership Legacy.

Website sources:
http://www..rleadershiplegacy.com/assessment/assessment.php

The Teal Trust (2001), Leadership Style Indicator

Website sources: www.teal.org.uk

Team Technology (1995) Mental Muscle Diagram Indicator

Website source: http://www.metarasa.com/resources/mmdi-report/

Benninga, J. S., Berkowitz, M. W., Kuehn, P., & Smith, K. (2006). Character and Academics:

What Good Institutions Do? Phi Delta Kappan, 87(6), 448-452. Retrieved from EBSCOhost.

Notes:

Notes:

Notes:

www.ingramcontent.com/pod-product-compliance
Lightning Source LLC
Chambersburg PA
CBHW070554220526
45467CB00003B/1207